I0882327

"Investigating healthcare fraud is a challenge for both the rookie and experienced investigator. Success requires knowledge of how our healthcare system works and of the broad range of potential fraud schemes unique to healthcare, along with solid investigative techniques and skills. Charles Piper's excellent book, *Healthcare Fraud Investigation Guidebook* covers all of these topics and more, providing investigators with the practical information they need to meet the challenge. A copy of Charles Piper's *Healthcare Fraud Investigation Guidebook* should be on every healthcare fraud investigator's desk."

Louis Saccoccio, JD
Chief Executive Officer
National Health Care Anti-Fraud Association

"Healthcare fraud is so enormous that no one can accurately estimate what the total cost is. And, it costs all of us. Everyone reading this sentence is the victim of healthcare fraud through higher medical fees, increased premiums, and tax hikes. I am grateful that an experienced fraud examiner such as Charles Piper has taken the time to share his extensive knowledge and experience so that others can join him in the fight to reduce this massive epidemic."

James D. Ratley
Chief Financial Officer, Chief Executive Officer, and President
Association of Certified Fraud Examiners

"Healthcare fraud is costing money and lives. Charles Piper's *Healthcare Fraud Investigation Guidebook* exposes the problem and provides tested methods to investigate healthcare shenanigans. *'The Piper Method'* of conducting thorough and complete investigations needs to become the preventive remedy that cures the greed that is poisoning the healthcare industry."

Scott Amey, JD
General Counsel
Project On Government Oversight (POGO)

"Whether you are working your first healthcare fraud case, or you are an experienced veteran, the *Healthcare Fraud Investigation Guidebook* by Charles E. Piper, CFE, will be your lifeline to a thorough, organized, and successful inquiry. Piper shares his decades of expertise to help you identify the fraud schemes and the investigative strategies used to best uncover them. Far more than an introduction to the topic, it is an encyclopedia on how healthcare fraud works, how to get to the bottom of it, and of particular value, how to look for fraud patterns so your investigations might be expanded beyond single providers and other wrongdoers. This book should be required reading for any fraud fighter investigating healthcare fraud."

Gilbert R. Jimenez, JD, CIG, LPD
Licensed Illinois Private Investigator

Principal
Insight Investigation Services of Chicago, Illinois

Attorney
Former Deputy Inspector General, Illinois

"Charles Piper's *Healthcare Fraud Investigation Guidebook* should be considered the *go-to* book for investigating healthcare fraud. His shared detailed investigative approach will help investigators to not only identify healthcare fraud, waste, and abuse but to also connect the dots and identify more fraud and more wrongdoers and then make recommendations for improvement to prevent reoccurrences. Piper's thorough and complete investigative methodology should be the standard practice for all investigators and investigative agencies and organizations. Taxpayers and all who pay insurance premiums will also be delighted that this revolutionary approach is being utilized to help make healthcare more affordable."

Bruce Durbin
(Retired) Federal Special Agent
U.S. Department of Homeland Security

"I worked closely with Charles Piper when we served as federal agents with the Defense Criminal Investigative Service. He is the consummate professional. Piper's *Healthcare Fraud Investigation Guidebook* is a great tool and resource for those responsible for investigating and prosecuting healthcare fraud. I highly recommend it."

Richard Zott
(Retired) Special Agent in Charge
U.S. Department of Defense

"Fraud fighter Charles Piper has hit another home run! In his *Healthcare Fraud Investigation Guidebook,* Piper has successfully dissected what many believe to be the most complicated venue of the investigative discipline. He presents healthcare fraud investigating into concise, easy-to-follow concepts that can be utilized by virtually anyone working in the field of healthcare administration, investigation, and prosecution. I highly recommend this book to all striving to identify and investigate healthcare fraud, waste, and abuse."

Gregory Mohr, CFS
(Retired) Federal Special Agent
Private Investigator and Security Consultant

Managing Director
Criminal Justice Training & Consulting, LLC

"Charles Piper worked for me as a Federal Senior Special Agent in Orlando, Florida. He was one of my smartest, most reliable, and hard-working agents. He always had the right investigative approach to identify, prove, and ultimately obtain convictions of his case subjects. The *Healthcare Fraud Investigation Guidebook* is reflective of Piper's knowledge and abilities to identify and investigate healthcare fraud. Many professional fraud fighters should benefit from this publication."

Richard L. Messersmith
(Retired) Resident Agent in Charge
Defense Criminal Investigative Service
Department of Defense Inspector General

(Retired) Special Agent
Air Force Office of Special Investigations

"Fraud is everywhere, but due to the unique nature of the healthcare industry, it provides even more opportunities for fraudulent actions by those with unscrupulous motives. To fight healthcare fraud, you have to understand what is *normal* in the business of medicine in order to recognize the *abnormal*. Charles Piper's *Healthcare Fraud Investigation Guidebook* has succeeded in providing the necessary groundwork as well as guidelines for the requirements that may be needed to successfully investigate various fraud in the healthcare industry."

Belinda M. Kitos, CFE, CICA, MLS (ASCP)
Certified Fraud Examiner

Certified Internal Controls Auditor

(Retired) Boarded Medical Laboratory Scientist
Specializing in Physician Medical Office Fraud

"I had the pleasure of working with Charles Piper, CFE, when we served as Federal Special Agents. He is always meticulous and persevering to dig out the truth. Piper's *Healthcare Fraud Investigation Guidebook* is filled with details on the many types of healthcare fraud schemes and his shared real-life War Stories are from the realities of the trenches. This book is a very useful tool for anyone investigating healthcare fraud."

Craig A. Brueckman, CFE
(Retired) Federal Special Agent

Investigative Consultant and Principal
Brueckman and Associates, LLC

"Having worked with Charles Piper, I know he conducts investigations with enthusiasm and passion. That same approach is shared in his latest book, *Healthcare Fraud Investigation Guidebook*. It is a must read for those conducting healthcare fraud investigations."

Thomas Terry, CFE
Private Investigator and Consultant

(Retired) U.S. Postal Inspector

Founder and Owner
Silent Service Financial Investigations

"Charles Piper has done it again! His *Healthcare Fraud Investigation Guidebook* is the complete 1, 2, 3 … A to Z guide on how to conduct healthcare fraud investigations. This book should be on every healthcare fraud investigator's desk."

Scott Baldwin
Owner and Private Investigator/Consultant
Advanced Investigative & Screening Solutions

"Healthcare fraud is not just conducted by providers but cuts across multiple disciplines, including: individuals, insurance providers, and hospitals. Charles Piper's *Healthcare Fraud Investigation Guidebook* provides an excellent focus on healthcare fraud and includes detailed examples and investigative guidance that healthcare investigators and auditors will greatly appreciate."

Durand Ferguson, CFE
Audit Manager
Memphis, Tennessee

"Having spent a career investigating fraud both within and beyond healthcare contexts, two things were crystal clear after reading Charles Piper's latest book, *Healthcare Fraud Investigation Guidebook.* First, Piper possesses significant fraud investigative experience, and a well-developed approach to fraud investigations. Second, his understanding of healthcare fraud is likely at a level few have attained in their careers. Consistent with his first book, *Investigator and Fraud Fighter Guidebook: Operation War Stories,* Piper uses his experience to teach the reader, starting with explaining the basics and terminology, up through planning and completing an entire fraud investigation, all the while weaving in first-hand examples of his fraud cases throughout the lessons. This is a must read book for anyone investigating fraud within healthcare contexts."

Stephen Pedneault, CPA/CFF, CFE
Founder
Forensic Accounting Services, LLC
Glastonbury, Connecticut

HEALTHCARE FRAUD INVESTIGATION GUIDEBOOK

HEALTHCARE FRAUD INVESTIGATION GUIDEBOOK

Charles E. Piper, CFE
Retired Federal Special Agent

CRC Press
Taylor & Francis Group
Boca Raton London New York

CRC Press is an imprint of the
Taylor & Francis Group, an **informa** business

CRC Press
Taylor & Francis Group
6000 Broken Sound Parkway NW, Suite 300
Boca Raton, FL 33487-2742

Version Date: 20160120

International Standard Book Number-13: 978-1-4987-5260-2 (Paperback)

Visit the Taylor & Francis Web site at
http://www.taylorandfrancis.com

and the CRC Press Web site at
http://www.crcpress.com

Contents

Preface

Doctors actually made house calls when I was growing up in the late 1950s and early 1960s on the South Side of Chicago. When I was sick (*or faking it to get out of going to school*), my mom would call the doctor's office from our rotary telephone in the kitchen while I would lay on the front room couch in my pajamas watching our black-and-white television. Soon the doctor arrived with his black leather satchel bag in hand. That's when I started getting scared. After my mom provided the doctor with a verbal description of my symptoms, he removed a stethoscope from his bag, pushed the cold end onto my chest, and told me to breathe in and out while he listened carefully through the stethoscope's earpieces. Then he'd stick a wooden stick down my throat and make me say, *"Ahhhhhhh,"* until I gagged. Next came the long look inside my ears where the doctor searched for something that he never did seem to find.

It seemed like our doctor's cure was always the same—a big needle and a long injection of penicillin. Maybe that was supposed to serve as a deterrent so I wouldn't fake being sick to get out of school. If so, it didn't work very well. Although I didn't like being around doctors as a kid, I still knew them to be trustworthy, honest, and caring professionals—just like the Chicago cops that patrolled our streets. *Except the cops didn't take crap from anyone.*

Little did I know then that house calls would soon be a thing of the past and a few decades later I'd be serving as a federal special agent conducting criminal and civil investigations of healthcare providers from coast to coast for committing millions of dollars in fraud.

Although most individuals that serve in the healthcare industry are dedicated, caring, and honest, it's also known that some unscrupulous "professional" providers scam the system, which often results in huge dollar losses to insurance companies, government programs, and taxpayers.

There are others who also rip off the healthcare industry, including the following:

- Patients and insurance beneficiaries
- Employers
- Insurance company employees and government insurance program employees
- Third-party administrators and fiscal intermediaries
- Fake business entities
- Organized crime groups (including street gangs)
- Hackers

Just in case you haven't been reading the newspapers, hackers are not just grown-ups that keep coughing up phlegm because they smoke too much. Hackers are those who wrongly, electronically penetrate and exploit the weaknesses in computer systems and networks. Medical ID fraud is causing all kinds of problems for patients, healthcare providers, and insurance companies.

Some have estimated that healthcare fraud in the United States results in losses of approximately $80 billion a year. It has been said that 80 billion one-dollar bills laid end-to-end would extend around the earth almost 320 times! Now that's a lot of loot!

There are additional indirect costs associated with healthcare fraud, including, but not limited to, the costs incurred to prevent and detect potential fraud, the costs to conduct investigations, and the costs for prosecutions and other remediation.

Sometimes, greed in the healthcare profession also results in quality of care issues. In other words, patients are sometimes neglected, hurt, or become worse because they are not receiving the quality of care they should. Patients sometimes endure care, treatments, and examinations that are not necessary. Some providers are being paid based on the quality and/or value of the care they provide rather than fees for services. Some of them just scam the system by doing less for the patients and are still getting paid.

During the 20 years I served as a federal agent and now as a private investigator and consultant, I have found that investigating healthcare fraud can be mentally and physically challenging. But I have also found it to be very rewarding.

I don't mean rewarding like you will make a lot of money (*although fraud fighters are often well paid*). I mean rewarding because it is fun taking down bad guys—especially when they are supposed to be good guys. When I say "guys," that also means gals because some of them commit fraud too.

Those who are new to investigating healthcare fraud are often seen at their desks scratching their heads in confusion or frustration while trying to learn or remember all of the fraud schemes, terms, and positions of professionals involved in healthcare and the healthcare insurance process. Some of the schemes have funny names like: "unbundling," "upcoding," "overutilization," and even "doctor shopping." But healthcare fraud investigators sometimes also get to work cases involving good ole' fashioned kickbacks and bribes.

Factually, investigating high-dollar healthcare fraud can sometimes be a bit confusing. Perhaps that's why my personal favorite scheme to investigate is the easy to prove "billing for services not rendered." Even a half-asleep jury can understand those types of false claims.

There are several useful books available on analytics, data mining, and detecting healthcare fraud. In fact, if you are a healthcare fraud investigator or examiner, I highly recommend that you read some of them. However, this book takes you to the next level. It not only assists in identifying healthcare fraud schemes, but it also provides helpful instructional guidance on how to investigate those fraudsters so that their wrongdoings can more likely be proven *beyond a reasonable doubt* and/or by the *preponderance of evidence*. This causes wrongdoers to be held accountable and wrongly obtained funds to be recouped through fines and judgments.

This book also emphasizes the importance of simultaneously searching for waste and abuse as well as systemic weaknesses and deficiencies that caused or contributed to the problem or wrongdoing under investigation and to then make recommendations for improvement.

The objective of this book is not to just put a Band-Aid on the problem of healthcare fraud but to actually try and cure it! Those tasked with the responsibility of investigating healthcare fraud should also be striving to improve the healthcare and payment systems not only by investigating fraudulent activity but by also striving to detect and deter other future instances of fraud, waste, and abuse.

During my career, I have investigated many different types of complex white collar crimes. But the majority of the healthcare fraud investigations I have conducted involved healthcare providers or their employers and organizations. Although organized crime is responsible for many high-dollar losses in healthcare fraud, it has been my experience that in total, healthcare providers are responsible for most or at least a large portion of the dollars lost due to fraud.

From an investigative standpoint, there are many things to consider when investigating healthcare providers as compared to investigating nonproviders. This book gives particular attention to the investigation of healthcare providers. It is my belief that once you learn how to successfully investigate healthcare provider fraud, investigating nonproviders (usually for lower-dollar amounts) is much easier. Plus, all or most of the same types of planning skills, tools, sources, resources, and techniques used when investigating providers can also be utilized and/or considered when investigating others. However, it is worth noting that investigating organized crime and hackers will require additional assistance from those who are specially trained to investigate these areas of crime, preferably law enforcement.

You may have read another crime-fighting book I wrote entitled *Investigator and Fraud Fighter Guidebook: Operation War Stories.** If not, I highly recommend that you consider reading it because the pages detail how to conduct thorough and complete investigations and actually solve more cases—with even fewer resources. The book includes many of my own personal War Stories and firsthand relevant experiences. It also details my own unique method of conducting investigations, which is called "The Piper Method of Conducting Thorough and Complete Investigations"* and includes a one-page diagram that outlines the method.

That same diagram of "The Piper Method"* follows. My unique method of conducting thorough and complete investigations is also detailed in this healthcare fraud investigation guidebook and recommended for use or consideration when conducting such investigations. I hope you will consider using this methodology (or at least elements of it) in your future investigations so that you might enjoy the same investigative success that I have, or even better results.

* Piper, Charles E., *Investigator and Fraud Fighter Guidebook: Operation War Stories*, John Wiley & Sons, Hoboken, NJ, 2014. (Copyright 2014, Wiley-VCH Verlag GmbH & Co. KGaA. Reproduced with permission.)

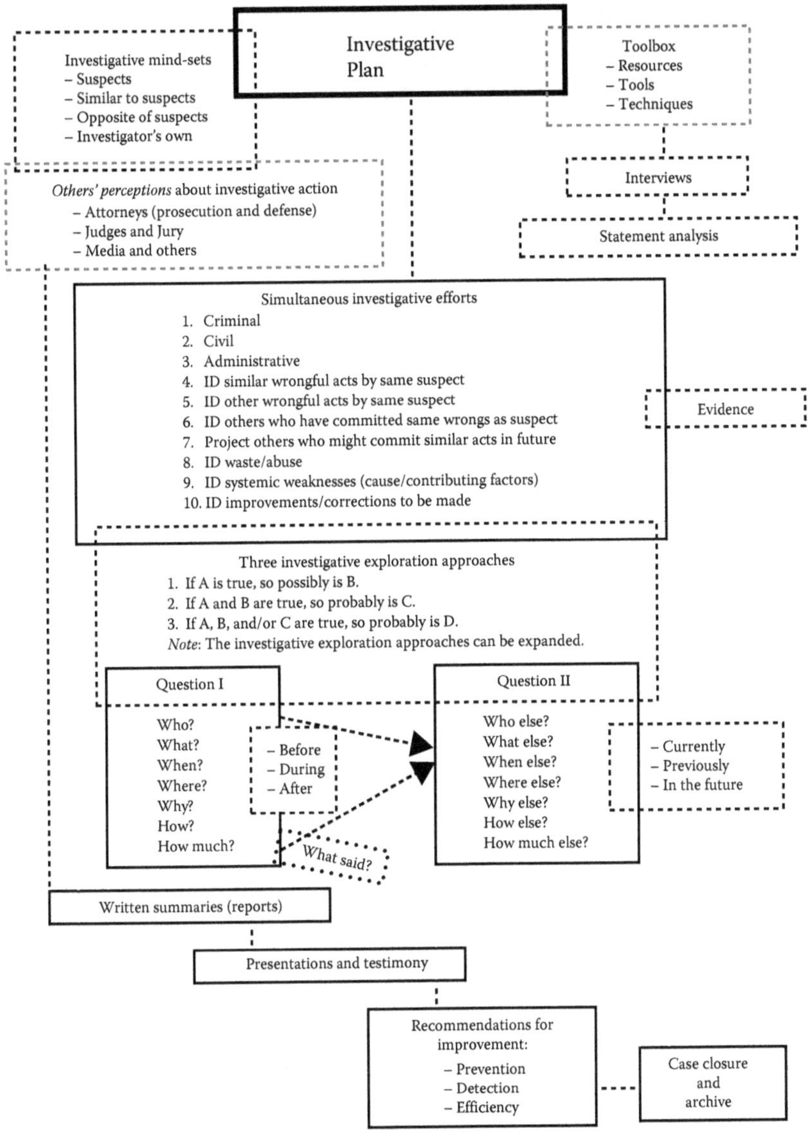

The "Piper Method" of conducting thorough and complete investigations. (From Piper, Charles E., *Investigator and Fraud Fighter Guidebook: Operation War Stories*, John Wiley & Sons, Hoboken, NJ, 2014. Copyright 2014, Wiley-VCH Verlag GmbH & Co. KGaA. Reproduced with permission.)

Acknowledgments

This book was written only because of the many opportunities I have had serving others, first as a member of the U.S. Army as a military policeman and investigator, then as a city police officer, a supervisory detective, a federal special agent–criminal investigator for 20 years, and now as a private investigator and consultant. During my career, I've had the pleasure of working with some of the finest law enforcement officers and investigators in the world. I am grateful for the comradery we have shared and the many friendships that I have developed.

Because of lessons learned over the years and my continued determination to stop criminal activity and other injustices, I have enjoyed a tremendous amount of success in the investigative profession. I have been lucky because more often than not I have had fun doing the job.

In my post–law enforcement career, I began writing to share my knowledge so that others might benefit from my lessons learned over the years. The positive feedback and recognition received from those books and articles led me to write this book for which I would like to express my sincere appreciation to the following.

The Association of Certified Fraud Examiners (ACFE), including Dr. Joseph Wells, Jim Ratley, Dick Carozza, and the entire crew at the ACFE.

I'm grateful to all of the dedicated healthcare and other fraud fighters I have had the pleasure of working with over the years, including federal agents and auditors from various law enforcement agencies (particularly the Department of Defense, Health and Human Services, the Federal Bureau of Investigation, the U.S. Postal Inspection Service, and many others), state and private insurance investigators, the program integrity personnel at various government and private insurance programs (particularly TRICARE), and federal prosecutors in both the criminal and civil divisions (particularly in Orlando and Tampa, Florida; Las Vegas, Nevada; Nashville and Memphis, Tennessee; and attorneys with the Department of Justice in Washington, DC).

I thank my wife and daughters, older brother, and other family members for all of their support and encouragement along the way.

I thank the publisher, CRC Press/Taylor & Francis, particularly Carolyn Spence, senior acquisitions editor; Jessica Vega, editorial assistant; Delroy Lowe, project coordinator; Linda Leggio, project editor; Shayna Murry, cover designer; Arunkumar Aranganathan of SPi Global; and all others who made this book possible.

Special thanks to John Wiley & Sons, the publisher of my first investigation textbook titled, *Investigator and Fraud Fighter Guidebook: Operation War Stories* for granting permission for select portions of that book to be included in this book, *Healthcare Fraud Investigation Guidebook*. Thank you also to the other agencies and organizations that granted permission for allowing other valued information to be included in this writing especially: the Association of Certified Fraud Examiners, the National Health Care Anti-Fraud Association, the Project On Government Oversight (POGO), and all others.

I would also like to thank the readers of this book. I hope my suggested investigative guidance, tips, and shared experiences will benefit you in the effort to not to just put a Band-Aid on the problem of healthcare fraud but to actually try to cure it.

Author

Charles E. Piper, CFE, CRT, is an award-winning investigator and author. He served for more than 30 years in law enforcement, including 20 years as a special agent–criminal investigator with the Department of Defense, where he conducted major fraud investigations from coast to coast. Piper has investigated numerous healthcare providers and others for fraud and worked jointly with federal special agents from the FBI and the many Offices of Inspector General. His investigations have resulted in millions of dollars in recoveries and criminal convictions and civil judgments against fraudsters. He is also a proud veteran of the U.S. Army.

Piper is currently the owner of Charles Piper's Professional Services in West Tennessee, which provides investigative, consulting, and training services. He is a Certified Fraud Examiner (CFE), Certified in the Reid Technique of Interview and Interrogation (CRT), and a graduate of three law enforcement investigative academies (federal, state, and military).

Piper has received numerous awards and recognition while serving in law enforcement, including Special Agent of the Year. Since opening his own company, Piper was the recipient of the 2014 ACFE Hubbard Award. He has written several anti-fraud and investigative articles for ACFE's *Fraud Magazine* and other publications.

In 2014, Piper authored the *Investigator and Fraud Fighter Guidebook: Operation War Stories** to assist investigators around the globe. The book introduced, "The Piper Method of Conducting Thorough and Complete Investigations."* This unique methodology can help investigators solve more cases and detect, prevent, and reduce criminal activity and other wrongdoings, as well as waste and abuse. This method is also used in his approach to investigating healthcare fraud and is provided here in the *Healthcare Fraud Investigation Guidebook.*

* Piper, Charles E., *Investigator and Fraud Fighter Guidebook: Operation War Stories,* John Wiley & Sons, Hoboken, NJ, 2014. (Copyright 2014, Wiley-VCH Verlag GmbH & Co. KGaA. Reproduced with permission.)

Piper is a member of the following organizations:

- The Association of Certified Fraud Examiners
- The Federal Law Enforcement Officers Association
- The Reid Institute
- The Tennessee Association of Investigators

For more information, visit www.piper-pi.com.

Charles E. Piper, CFE, CRT (Retired Federal Special Agent)

(Photo courtesy of Ben Hubbard.)

chapter one

Background on healthcare insurance and related fraud

Growth of healthcare insurance in America

This chapter does not contain a complete history about healthcare insurance in America. But the glimpse provided shows that the U.S. government and state governments (meaning the taxpayers) pay a lot of money to ensure that most Americans have or can gain access to affordable or free healthcare.

Healthcare coverage during World War II

The United States experienced a sudden large increase in employer sponsored healthcare coverage during World War II (1939–1945). Because of a shortage of workers and increased demand for goods, the federal government implemented a freeze on wages to prevent workers from repeatedly changing jobs. But the government said that fringe benefits were not considered wages and could therefore be offered to employees.

Those fringe benefits included things like sick leave and employer sponsored healthcare plans. After the private sector started providing employer sponsored health insurance, more public organizations started offering it too. As a result, many employees that previously did not have insurance suddenly received coverage and their employers paid for most or all of the premiums (annual payments). But because not everyone was employed (some couldn't find jobs, some were disabled, and so forth), everyone still did not have healthcare insurance.

Medicare and Medicaid

In 1965, individuals with low incomes and the elderly (over age 65) got breaks when President Lyndon Johnson signed the Medicare and Medicaid programs into law. Later, people with disabilities were allowed to apply to be considered for Medicare too. But Medicare doesn't always cover 100 percent of all of the costs associated with care. Therefore, many people purchase supplemental policies to help cover the costs. Medicaid also helps pay the costs of healthcare for those with low incomes and is run by individual states. Funding for Medicaid comes from those individual states and the federal government.

As a result of efforts by President George W. Bush, in January 2006, Medicare Part D was implemented. It helps to pay at least some of the costs of prescription drugs for recipients that enroll in the plan.

Author's Note: *It's worth noting that under the current law, Medicare cannot negotiate discounts with drug manufacturers to reduce the government's expense for Medicare prescriptions, which results in higher costs to U.S. taxpayers. Ironically, the Department of Veterans Affairs and TRICARE (both mentioned in the text that follows), as well as Medicaid are all permitted to negotiate such discounts.*

Affordable Care Act

On March 23, 2010, President Barack Obama signed the Affordable Care Act (ACA) (commonly called "Obama Care") into law. As a result, many Americans who previously could not afford healthcare insurance have been able to obtain coverage. For many (especially those with lower incomes), healthcare became affordable because of income-based federal tax subsidies (tax credits). Debates about whether the federal government should be paying such subsidies will no doubt continue. In fact, repealing the ACA is on many politicians' agendas.

Factually, many restrictions were lifted as a result of the ACA, which benefitted many Americans. For example, insurance companies' right to refuse to cover people with preexisting conditions was removed. Lifetime care financial caps were also removed. Children under age 26 can remain on their parents' insurance policies.

Many said that individual and employee healthcare insurance premiums would not increase as a result of implementing the ACA. But factually, some premiums did increase. Promises were made that employees would be able to keep their current employer sponsored coverage (and "keep their own doctor") after the ACA was implemented. Yet, many employees actually lost their employer coverage or couldn't keep their own doctor.

In the developmental stages of the ACA, it was announced that not long after implementing the ACA, employers that offered healthcare insurance plans that cost individuals or families over a specified dollar amount would have to pay a 40 percent excise tax on the dollar amount that exceeds the threshold. Understandably, many employers were not very happy about that and immediately started making adjustments.

After the ACA was implemented, some individuals' healthcare insurance premiums remained the same or dropped in price. At the surface that sounds like good news. However, some insurance plans shifted the costs to the beneficiaries in other ways including increasing annual deductibles that healthcare recipients must pay before their insurance would actually kick in. Another way that costs were shifted was by increasing the co-payments that healthcare recipients must pay each time they visited the doctor. Some co-payments have increased by 50 percent or more. Therefore, some annual "premiums" may have remained unchanged or may have been reduced, but the overall "cost" to some healthcare recipients each year has actually increased.

Many employers also offer their employees the opportunity to contribute to health savings accounts in which the employees can pay for eligible healthcare with tax-free dollars. This sounds like a nice perk. But all it means is that the money the employees already earned and put into their own healthcare savings accounts is not taxed when those funds are used for "eligible" healthcare costs. It's not like the employees didn't already earn that money in the first place. These less expensive premiums with higher deductibles are called "Consumer Directed Health Plans."

So, if an employee or other healthcare recipient stays very healthy (or doesn't seek medical care), their out-of-pocket costs might remain about the same as before ACA. But if they get sick often or have some major health problem for which they seek medical care, it might cost them more than they were paying before the ACA.

Prior to the ACA, many employers (including federal, state, and local governments) guaranteed their retirees that their insurance premiums would be covered in a manner previously agreed to. However, with the escalating healthcare premium prices (*and because of historic mismanagement of government funds*), some cash-strapped municipalities (and other employers) have strived to eliminate or reduce coverage previously promised to retirees and their spouses and other family members. Understandably, those retirees opposed such efforts and feel their previous employers have broken their promises.

Remember how I said that ACA allowed children to stay on their parents' insurance policies until they turn 26 years old? Well, almost predictably, many employers and insurance companies have made adjustments to that provision to decrease their own expenses.

Beginning in 2015, some started charging additional fees for employees' dependent spouses and adult children who have access to healthcare insurance from their own employers. Some policies will continue to cover the employee, but if their spouse or adult children can obtain healthcare insurance from their own employers, they will be required to do so (if they still want insurance). This in effect causes the families to pay more out of their own pockets for healthcare coverage than they did before ACA. Sure it's great that dependents can stay on their parents' health insurance until age 26—but for many it's at an additional cost.

Author's Note: *For most Americans, healthcare is not cheap, it's not affordable and it's not free. Debates are sure to continue about what should and should not be done to best serve the American people and the country. Changes should be anticipated.*

Department of Veterans Affairs

In 2014, the Department of Veterans Affairs (VA) that provides healthcare (usually at no cost) to U.S. military veterans found itself in a reported scandal involving cover-ups regarding the length of time it took to schedule medical appointments as well as the quality of care. It was reported that some patients might have died while waiting extended for periods of time for treatment. The federal government then set aside funding to allow veterans to obtain healthcare outside VA channels (at the government's expense) if they could not be seen in a timely fashion, and for those who lived far from VA facilities. That "fix" has reportedly not worked out so well for many veterans.

Author's Note: *It's also worth noting that veterans who have additional private insurance coverage who receive healthcare at VA facilities may find that their other insurance plans will be billed for services provided by the VA. In other words, the VA not only receives funding from tax dollars but also receives funds for services provided from private insurance companies. Many veterans who are not retired from the military and who do not have recognized service-connected disabilities often complain that they cannot receive care from the VA because they reportedly earn too much.*

TRICARE

Others that obtain government-paid healthcare include active duty military members and their dependents and military retirees. They can receive care through a program called TRICARE.

Author's Note: *There are many other government-sponsored or affiliated programs and private insurance companies. Some employers even insure their own employees. Some individuals may have healthcare insurance coverage from more than one source. For example, they may have coverage through Medicare, TRICARE, or perhaps through a private insurance policy. Some are enrolled in Medicare and Medicaid. Many of those who have multiple insurance coverage plans pay little or nothing out of their own pockets for their medical expenses. As an investigator, you should keep in mind that more than one insurance company or government insurance program can become victimized by a fraudster's false billings involving a single patient who has coverage through multiple insurance plans or programs.*

Bait-and-switch and automatic renewal insurance policies

Perhaps, it's not actually an intended "bait-and-switch" tactic, but many healthcare insurance companies drastically change their policies each year. In other words, what's covered and the dollar amounts covered can vary greatly from year to year. Also, sometimes coverage for specific drugs may drastically change. Premiums can also increase from year to year.

How will the healthcare beneficiaries know about the changes? They have to study the plans carefully before their policies are scheduled for automatic renewal. Doing nothing usually results in automatic renewal. Yet, changes to coverage may have been made that the beneficiary assumed would be the same as the previous year. Experts suggest that healthcare recipients should study all offered plans to find out which ones are best for the individual patient.

Author's Note: *For many individuals, purchasing and maintaining healthcare coverage is almost like having to go out looking to rent a new apartment every single year because your landlord might decide to double your rent, take away your parking privileges, or decide your pet deposit fees will triple. Some might entice the renters to move in immediately and get 1 month free, but when you read the renter's agreement you'll find it's not as beneficial in the long run. In short, healthcare beneficiaries must study much more than how much their annual premiums will cost before deciding on which policy is best for them. In fairness, some insurance policies might actually increase benefits at lesser costs. (Let us all know when you find those.) There is one thing you can be certain of and that is that politicians on both sides of the aisle will continue to fight for and against healthcare coverage and costs that directly impact not only your pocketbook but also your health. Time has shown that there is much partisanship as battles continue among politicians, political supporters, certain industries, special interest groups, and individuals. Make no mistake about it—your vote matters.*

Medicare has a "Medicare Plan Finder" on its website. Medicare recipients will need to enter at least their own zip code to search for the best plan. For additional information, visit: https://www.medicare.gov/find-a-plan/questions/home.aspx.

As stated, this chapter does not contain a complete history on healthcare insurance in America. This glimpse, however, shows that the U.S. government and state governments (meaning the taxpayers) pay a lot of money to ensure that most Americans have or can gain access to affordable or free healthcare. As a result, many employees in the healthcare and insurance arenas have good and even lucrative jobs. Many hospitals, companies, and other entities also rake in big bucks—including the ones that are considered "nonprofit."

For-profit versus nonprofit providers

Some healthcare entities (including hospitals) are considered "for profit" and some are considered "nonprofit." For many years, I thought nonprofit meant that everyone who worked at the nonprofit facility either donated their time as volunteers or worked for peanuts and their goal was to provide their services at minimal costs. Let me emphasize that is *not* even close to being accurate.

Some of the best paid executives, employees, medical staff, and contractors work for "nonprofit" entities, which include hospitals. In fact, some nonprofit hospitals might charge more than for-profit hospitals for the same exact types of care, services, medication, bandages, or even aspirin.

For-profit hospitals share profits with their stockholders and owners. Nonprofits do not have stockholders or owners to share "additional funds" with. Instead, they often use those funds to expand their efforts by building more wings or buildings, hiring more physicians, buying more equipment, or giving their employees pay raises. Feel free to do your own research on the differences between for-profit and nonprofit. Just don't assume that because a hospital is "nonprofit," the hospital and its employees or executives would not have a motive to charge high prices or commit fraud.

Recent healthcare fraud investigations

The Department of Justice (DOJ) reported that the Medicare Strike Force set new records for prosecutions in fiscal year 2013. The strike force is often referred to as the "Heat Task Force" (Health Care Fraud Prevention and Enforcement Action Team). The DOJ also flaunted that for every dollar that the DOJ and the U.S. Department of Health and Human Services spent fighting fraud, they returned an average of $8 to the government. Most of those fraud-fighting efforts have been focused on nine cities (Baton Rouge, Louisiana; Brooklyn, New York; Chicago, Illinois; Dallas, Texas; Detroit, Michigan; Houston, Texas; Los Angeles, California; Miami, Florida; and Tampa, Florida). It was reported that in fiscal year 2013, the DOJ recovered $3.8 billion in civil fraud cases. In early 2014, the DOJ also reported that the Medicare Strike Force charged more than 1700 defendants since 2007.

So, fighting fraud can apparently reap a good return on investment. But don't forget that the fraud prevention and detection efforts are actually incorporated into the cost of healthcare fraud. Factually, fraudsters are responsible for more losses than will ever be precisely quantified. Since fighting healthcare fraud can be so lucrative for the government, many wonder why the number of cities focused on is so limited.

The author's experience investigating healthcare providers

My introduction to investigating healthcare fraud came in the early 1990s while serving as a federal agent with the Department of Defense. The cases I worked for the feds prior to that were other types of complex white collar cases such as product substitution, defective products, contract and procurement fraud, and bribery and corruption.

Because of working those other time-consuming, paper-intensive, and usually analytical-type investigations, I already knew how to plan and conduct long-term investigations. I always strove to use the best and most appropriate investigative tools and resources to get the job done, wrote detailed summary reports, conducted detailed interviews, briefed criminal and civil prosecutors, made presentations, and testified in court when necessary. I knew the importance of staying organized when conducting white collar fraud investigations that involved voluminous sets of records and documents.

However, I found that healthcare fraud was a horse of a different color. Suddenly, I had to learn the meaning of healthcare acronyms such as CPT Codes,* EOBs,† HMOs,‡ and PPOs.§ I also had to try to figure out what information was important to my case and what wasn't. Like investigating the other types of fraud, I learned once again that it's easy to feel overwhelmed by it all.

I must confess that initially my heart and soul didn't want to believe that professional healthcare providers would knowingly and intentionally submit claims for payment, which they knew were false. I guess I wanted to think of all of the providers as being honest and caring just like all of the ones I knew (or thought I knew) from the past. But like the other types of fraud investigated, I quickly learned that all too often, many healthcare providers do commit fraud. In fact, the amount of dollars lost to healthcare fraud is sickening.

It's sometimes estimated that between 3 and 10 percent of business dollars are lost due to fraud. I believe that's a conservative estimate. In 2010, it was estimated that health expenditures in the United States reached almost $2.6 trillion. Since then, estimates by the Centers for Medicare and Medicaid Services and others projected annual increases of over 7 percent a year. National healthcare spending for 2019 is estimated at $4.5 trillion.

The first few healthcare fraud investigations I conducted in the 1990s were pursued while learning on the fly. Most of the other special agent

* CPT Codes—Current Procedural Terminology

† EOB—Explanation of Benefits

‡ HMO—Health Maintenance Organization

§ PPO—Preferred Provider Organization

investigators in my office had not yet investigated any healthcare cases and most didn't want to. Once I started working one of those cases, it seemed like most of the new healthcare fraud referrals that came in ended up on my desk too. However, it wasn't long before almost every agent in my office also had a few healthcare fraud investigations in their open-case inventory. In time, those other agents and I all started attending training to improve our knowledge about healthcare fraud—mostly healthcare provider fraud. We didn't investigate many individual patients or beneficiaries for fraud because the dollar losses were too low. But we did investigate some. Usually, we only investigated high-dollar loss cases. It was our experience that providers of care as well as hospitals and business entities were most often responsible for the *big bucks* fraud.

I quickly learned that there are more ways to defraud healthcare insurance companies and government programs than to cook shrimp. It's important for investigators to know the different types of fraud schemes because very often the crooked healthcare providers commit more than one type of fraud to profit illegally. Sometimes, the offenses you start out investigating are just the tip of the iceberg.

Kickbacks and corruption are also very common in the healthcare industry. I think all investigators enjoy investigating bribery and corruption cases. There's a gratifying feeling of accomplishment when taking down a government or private sector employee who compromises their integrity for personal profit or to the exclusion of fair and open competition. I mention this because I next want to share with you a very valuable tip that I received about how to uncover corruption. I learned this while attending a training program on procurement fraud. The instructor was an experienced federal white collar investigator who said, "The best place to develop a corruption case is to look on your desk."

Most of us in the classroom were initially confused by the instructor's suggestion. But he continued by saying something like, "If you are investigating a product substitution case, a defective product case, a bid-rigging case, or any other major contract fraud case, you know that the people who committed those types of offenses have no morals. If they are willing to commit those types of offenses, they probably would also be willing to pay bribes and kickbacks."

The point is, when conducting healthcare fraud or any other investigations, you must keep an eye out for the other wrongdoing that the same suspects are involved in. Sometimes, the other wrongs that you'll identify are more serious than what you started out investigating.

When you uncover many different types of fraud and corruption schemes, it makes those cases even more appealing to prosecutors to accept for prosecution for several reasons. First, you'll have demonstrated the suspects are serious fraudsters and didn't just make some honest mistakes. Second, because of identifying the additional wrongdoing, you will have no doubt identified increased dollar losses, which will often result in larger dollar recoveries. Third, you might also identify more victims. Plus, if your case results in a criminal conviction or civil judgment with a large dollar recovery, there will probably be a pretty nice press release where all prosecutors, investigators, examiners, and auditors will receive credit and publicity for the results of their hard work.

WAR STORY 1.1

A partial hospitalization company I investigated in southwest Florida submitted numerous false insurance billing claims to government programs for reimbursement, which were subsequently paid. The most outrageous scheme they had going was billing for "group therapy" of Alzheimer's patients. The staff made the patients gather in front of a large-screen television to repeatedly watch the movie, "*Forrest Gump.*" Granted it's a great movie, but billing for group therapy for making the patients watch it over and over didn't quite pass the "smell test." The investigation of this and other schemes committed by the same entity resulted in a $6 million recovery.

WAR STORY 1.2

I investigated a mental health service provider's facility in Little Rock, Arkansas, for a variety of different healthcare fraud schemes but they also utilized a slick method of acquiring new patients. I'll call this company, Counselors R Us. The owners had a second landline telephone installed at the their office's front desk, and the phone number was assigned to a fictitious referral service called something like AAA Mental Health Counseling Referral Service. The owners also placed an advertisement in the city phone book. You may have guessed that the triple-A name was created so that they'd be listed first in the phone directory under the mental health counseling category.

When the new phone rang, the receptionist was instructed by the owners to disguise her voice and inquire about the caller's problem and more importantly to ask if the caller had insurance. If the caller did not have insurance, the receptionist gave them the telephone number of the state's mental health facility. If they did have insurance, the receptionist gave the caller the phone number to Counselors R Us.

A few minutes later, when the caller telephoned Counselors R Us, the receptionist spoke in her normal voice and acted like she knew nothing at all about the previous call and referral. I think you'll agree that this was an ingenious (but unethical) way to bring in new business. However, there was so much healthcare fraud going on inside that facility that the phone referral scheme was just the tip of the iceberg.

By the way, when I interviewed the receptionist, I asked her to give me a vocal demo of her disguised voice when answering the referral telephone line. During her low-pitched performance, I had to bite my tongue to keep a straight face. The receptionist went on to tell me she didn't like the assignment but was just trying to keep her job. This is a typical truthful response of employees who are sometimes almost forced to assist in their employers' fraud schemes.

WAR STORY 1.3

While in Las Vegas, Nevada, I investigated an allergy clinic for providing an experimental allergy drug treatment that was not approved by the Food and Drug Administration, and therefore, not reimbursable by government health insurance programs. To unjustly get reimbursed for the experimental treatment, the owner of the clinic, who was also an allergy doctor, miscoded the treatment on the insurance claim forms by using a different code that was acceptable and reimbursable.

Although this fraud scheme was very profitable for the owner, it was subsequently discovered that the same facility was involved in an even larger dollar fraud scheme in which claims were submitted for allergy injections that were never given at all. Worse yet, the facility inflated the number and frequency that unique "mixtures" of antigens were created for each individual patient. Injections were reimbursable at about $50 a pop but the unique mixtures were billed at much more and resulted in even higher-dollar false claims.

These War Stories demonstrate a few types of fraud schemes and the importance of not creating tunnel vision when investigating healthcare fraud (or any other fraud). Remember, if the suspects are committing one type of fraud, they are probably committing other types and don't rule out the fact that they might also be receiving or paying bribes or kickbacks. When conducting any type of investigation, *think plural, not singular.*

Providers

Human providers

Healthcare providers (at least as referred to in this book) include but are not limited to general practitioners (all medical doctors), surgeons, allergists, podiatrists, anesthesiologists, ophthalmologists, neurologists, mental health providers, chiropractors, dentists, physical therapists, pharmacists, nurses, physician assistants, laboratory scientists, and so on.

Brick & mortar and mobile providers

Other "providers" include businesses, companies, and corporations. These may include but are not limited to medical and psychiatric hospitals, medical clinics, nursing homes, clinic labs, mobile labs, pharmacies, and so on. And let's not forget the facilities that provide x-rays, electrocardiograms, magnetic resonance imaging, ultrasounds, and all those other "electronic look inside" or measuring providers. There are also the suppliers of durable medical equipment, bandages, and other items that are shipped to patients and healthcare facilities; as well as ambulance transportation service providers and others.

All insurance is not equal

Many people assume that their healthcare insurance policy covers "everything." A common overconfident reply is, "Yes, I have health insurance." But some later learn that they don't have as much coverage as they thought. They may find that their policy does not cover (or they have limited coverage on) dental (including braces), vision (including frames and antireflective coating), or they may have no coverage on other items that the assumed were included. They may learn that they only have coverage for a few days stay at a hospital (*Ouch!*).

Some policies require the patient to only see the particular providers that the insurance company assigns—these are called Health Maintenance Organizations. Some policies inform beneficiaries that they can only see providers in their own insurance company's network. These are called Preferred Provider Organizations. If the patient deviates from this requirement when selecting a provider, they may be on the hook to pay all, most, or more of the costs out of their own pocket.

Many policies require precertification for hospitalization before the insurance kicks in (starts paying for the services). Failure to provide the precertification in advance could result in the patient (or beneficiary) paying for some or all of the costs incurred.

In short, the type of insurance one has (or lacks) makes a big difference. Many policies also have annual deductibles, which the beneficiary must pay each year before their insurance kicks in. Many also require the patient to pay a co-payment each time they visit a doctor or receive a healthcare service. One theory on the need for co-payments is that if the insurance company requires the patient to pay something, the patient won't keep running to the doctor every time they have the slightest thing wrong or they might take better care of themselves.

Different billable rates by insurance companies and government healthcare programs

Insurance companies are known to negotiate separate fee schedules with providers (or at least those providers that agree to be in their network) and they negotiate a lower rate than what the provider ordinarily charges for the services. In other words, in many cases, those providers can and do bill those insurance companies less than they would charge someone without insurance. The insured patient then receives an additional benefit because the dollar amount the patient pays is even less because the insurance company pays its share.

Those without insurance are usually the ones who can least afford to pay higher prices. It's almost hard to believe that someone without insurance often gets billed a higher rate for the same treatment as someone who has insurance. Obviously, someone that does not have healthcare insurance (i.e., not covered by a government program like Medicaid or Medicare) can get hit financially twice: (1) the uninsured pay the provider's higher rate (because it was not reduced through negotiations with the insurance company) and (2) the uninsured have to pay all of the cost because they don't have an insurance company to cover any of the cost.

Some hospitals might offer the uninsured discounts from their list prices. The process can sometimes be like negotiating a discount from the sticker price when you are buying a new car. If you don't ask for the discount, you might not get it. A few states have reportedly taken steps to ensure that hospitals cannot charge the uninsured more than what Medicare pays.

Medicare and Medicaid usually pay providers the least dollar amount for services. Medicaid often pays less than Medicare. It's been suggested that those prices are closer to the actual costs. Providers know in advance what those programs will pay and some agree in advance to accept the lower-dollar amounts. This arrangement must still be profitable because many providers advertise that they want Medicare patients to come to their facilities. But if they are making a profit by treating lower-cost Medicare patients, why do providers charge everyone else so much more?

The answer is simply, "because they can." One thing is certain, the rules, laws, policies, and prices will continue to change.

When investigating healthcare provider fraud, always remember that healthcare in America is a business. Although some healthcare providers might participate in some charitable work, by and large the cash register bells ring every time a customer (also known as a patient) is seen. When fraud occurs, sometimes the cash register bells ring even when the patients are not seen.

The next chapter describes 20 of the most common healthcare provider fraud schemes and identifies some unique red flags.

chapter two

Twenty common healthcare provider fraud schemes

This chapter details what I consider the 20 most common healthcare provider fraud schemes. During my professional career as a federal agent and now as a private investigator and consultant, I have successfully investigated or assisted others in investigating all 20 schemes (some more often than others). Keep in mind that your individual investigation may find more than one of the following schemes, and others. The schemes are listed here in alphabetical order.

Ambulance and transportation fraud

Ambulance and transportation fraud can occur in many different ways. One example is simply billing for patients that were never transported. Although a separate list of red flags is provided later in this chapter, it is worth noting here that if there are billings for ambulance rides on specified dates, there should also be billings for some types of examinations, treatments, or services for the same dates as the transports. But don't always assume that those billings for examinations, treatments, or services really happened as reported either. Of course, you will be conscious of the fact that an 11:45 PM ambulance ride on a Friday night might end up with a billing for an exam, treatment, or service on Saturday morning. It's the repeated pattern of finding no corresponding examinations, treatments, or services that indicates possible reoccurring fraud.

Another example of ambulance and transportation fraud is billing for more miles than actually driven. Taxi drivers have a bad reputation for this—perhaps leaving the meter running after the previous passenger exits or taking the long route to the hotel or airport. Hopefully, an ambulance driver is not taking a sightseeing tour on the way to the hospital.

Billing for noncovered services as covered services

Each insurance company and government program has a list of services they cover. They might also have a list of services they don't cover. Billing for noncovered services disguised as covered services occurs when a healthcare provider provides a service that is not covered, but then lists it on the claim form with a name (and/or code) for a service that is covered. An example of this might be when chiropractic services are not covered, so they are listed and billed as a massage or vice versa.

WAR STORY 2.1

As previously mentioned, I once investigated an allergy clinic for providing an experimental allergy treatment (injections) that was not approved by the Food and Drug Administration (FDA). The insurance company that received the claim forms for payment from the provider informed me that because the experimental treatment was not approved by the FDA, it was not reimbursable. The patient could have paid for the experimental treatment out of their own pocket if they wanted to, but the insurance company would not have knowingly paid the provider for non-FDA-approved treatment.

I reviewed the allergy clinic's website and found that it actually advertised that the clinic provided the experimental treatment. In fact, the website invited patients to come in and learn more about the treatment. Obviously, there was no question this treatment was made available to the clinic's patients.

After reviewing some patient files, I found a few instances where it was apparent that some patients received the experimental treatment and that the insurance company was regularly billed as if FDA-approved treatments (injections) were provided. I later drove to some of the patients' homes and interviewed them. They told me that the allergy doctor assured them that the experimental treatment would be covered by their insurance companies.

Based on the information obtained, I had tangible evidence (the patient records, the doctor's notes, the claim forms, and records of payment, which I received from the insurance company). I also had witness testimony (statements from the patients). The only thing that would make the case stronger was getting the allergy doctor to admit that she, knowing generated the miscoded and misleading claim forms, submitted them to the insurance company and received payment for the false claims. It would also be helpful to get a current or former employee to tell what they knew, observed, or heard. Needless to say, I only wanted the truth.

Well, almost predictably, a former employee cooperated and told me what she knew about the miscoding. This was damaging evidence against the provider. In addition, the allergy doctor subsequently admitted that she knew that she didn't follow the rules when generating the claim forms. The allergy doctor's defense was that the experimental treatment was effective and it was not her fault that the FDA took so long to approve useful treatment. From experience, I knew that almost all suspects who admit wrongdoing also attempt to justify their actions.

In this case, the allergy doctor submitted false claims for the experimental treatment to numerous insurance companies and government healthcare programs. Some allergy patients also had insurance coverage from more than one insurance program or company. In those instances, two or more insurance providers were defrauded for each patient. For example, one patient was retired from the military so he had TRICARE coverage, and because he was also over age 65 and retired he also had coverage from Medicare. The patient boasted that he seldom had to ever pay any out-of-pocket expenses for his healthcare because of having coverage by both TRICARE and Medicare.

Billing for services or items not provided

Almost every healthcare fraud investigation I have conducted has resulted in finding evidence that the provider also billed for services that were never provided. Even if the provider committed mostly different types of fraud schemes, evidence was also found that numerous claims for services were submitted, which had absolutely no supportive documentation.

From personal experience as a patient visiting doctors' offices, I knew that when a patient visits, at least one employee should always write something down. Even before the doctor comes in to see the patient, some staff member usually checks the patient's blood pressure and temperature and may even have them step on a scale to check their weight. Somebody should write down something and put the date on it (*granted today more records are maintained electronically so they might have typed it instead of writing it down*). As a fraud fighter, always be on the lookout for this scheme no matter what allegations you start out investigating. I will emphasize once again that you should always be looking for a repeated pattern of billing for services not rendered because that would indicate fraud.

A similar scheme occurs when a supplier fails to provide or ship items billed for. There are a lot of different subschemes that can be used to profit in this manner. For example, a company might be under obligation to provide powered wheelchairs, but instead, the company might provide nonpowered ones. That scheme is likely to be easily detected through patient complaints (*unless the patients are also in on the scheme*).

When investigating healthcare products, think along the lines of product substitution. For example, the patient or receiving entity might have ordered expensive high-quality widgets but, instead, they received inexpensive low-quality widgets. Quantity shortages are also a way to commit this type of fraud. It's especially easy when large quantities are supposed to be delivered. If an entity orders 500 or more of something, odds are that nobody is going to count each and every item.

"Ghost shipments" sounds kind of spooky doesn't it? That's when the company sends invoices for payment (sometimes even certifying that they shipped items) but they never shipped anything (except the invoice). This is a real problem in large bureaucratic organizations like the military. Sometimes, the people in the accounts payable section never talk to the people who work in the shipping and receiving department. And sometimes none of them talk to the contracting officers (or ordering officials), who awarded the contracts or placed the orders for the items.

WAR STORY 2.2

While conducting an investigation of a medical equipment supplier in Memphis, Tennessee, I learned that the contractor constantly billed for items that he never shipped. I also noticed all of that supplier's invoices read "Two Percent Net 30." That meant that the supplier offered the customer a two percent discount if payment was made within 30 days. The customer (located in Pennsylvania) was so eager to receive the discount that they always paid the invoices as soon as they were received. The problem was that the supplier wasn't shipping any goods.

During the investigation, I learned the customer's shipping and receiving department had a long list of complaints about the lack of items received and they wrote up numerous reports of discrepancy—which they called, "RODS." I asked one of the RODS clerks what they did when they learned a supplier didn't ship anything or shipped less than was requested. The clerk responded, "We call them on the phone and tell them to ship what they were supposed to."

I thought, no wonder the suppliers are playing the system. The worse that happens if they get caught committing fraud is to be told to do what they should have done in the first place. And when nobody complains the fraudster makes 100 percent profit. I later learned that the personnel in the RODS section never communicated with the contracting section and the contracting officers just kept awarding more and more contracts to the same supplier because that supplier had the lowest prices in the country. Of course, they had the lowest prices—they were not shipping anything.

WAR STORY 2.3

I interviewed one doctor who routinely billed for services that were never provided, which was evident by the lack of written entries in the patient files. When asked where all the missing documents were, the doctor blamed it on a flood. The doctor then changed stories and blamed it on a computer glitch. However, they could not explain why there were also no entries in the appointment calendar for the visits either. Some of the doctor's patients also told me they never visited the doctor's office on the dates where there was no documentation but claims were submitted. The patients' own verbal statements removed any wiggle room for the doctor.

Billing for unnecessary services, examinations, and tests

This scheme is sometimes referred to as "overutilization." This occurs when a patient receives services, tests, and/or examinations that are not necessary. Why would this happen?

Thinking like a fraud investigator, you could suspect that perhaps the physician, provider, technician, or business owner may be able to increase their profits by making the patient go through the cycle.

It's been suggested that doctors that own their own labs tend to bill for more lab testing than others, who do not own their own labs. Obviously, owning their own labs cuts out the middlemen and therefore increases internal profits. In other instances, there's also a strong possibility that there could be some kickback arrangement going on where the referring physician receives kickbacks from either the receiving entity or provider for referring patients for examinations and tests.

Many hospitals have found additional ways to legally increase their profits. In recent years, many hospitals have aligned themselves with private medical practice groups. There's an increasing trend in the number of physician practices that are actually owned by hospitals. It's been estimated that over 50 percent of physician practices are now owned by hospitals. Some hospitals even require the physicians associated with it to sign noncompete agreements where all of their patient referrals must go to their hospital. Many hospitals also have their own in-house labs. Therefore, those additional in-house tests can increase profits for the hospital.

There is another reason that excessive examinations and tests might be performed. Factually, hospitals, medical providers, and their practices get sued. Sometimes they are sued because they allegedly failed to properly diagnose a problem. Providers may require patients to undergo additional exams and tests simply to protect themselves from potential lawsuits. Factually, most providers (and their employers) pay for medical and other liability insurance. People filing lawsuits against them (founded or not) can cause providers' liability insurance premiums to increase. It almost stands to reason that some providers might require extra tests and exams to be performed on patients in a defensive effort to avoid lawsuits.

Obviously, it may be indicative of a fraud scheme when it can be proven that an extremely high percentage of patients are referred for the same type of examinations, which is not the industry norm. If you can show that the referring physician (or his/her employer or even better, an immediate family member) has a financial interest in the place receiving the referrals you might have just hit a home run. But proving fraud beyond reasonable doubt in a criminal case or even the preponderance of the evidence in a civil case is not an easy thing to do. Perhaps that's a good thing because we don't want to be formerly accusing people of wrongdoing if insufficient evidence exists. As this book will later show, witnesses (especially employees and former employees), who are willing to truthfully testify about such wrongdoing, can strengthen your cases when fraud actually occurred.

Billing when the provider is out of the office

This scheme is an *oldie but a goodie.* How can a provider bill for services when the provider is not even in the building where the services were said to have been provided? This actually happens all too often. Sure, sometimes dates can be written down or logged incorrectly but a pattern of this type is indicative of fraud.

WAR STORY 2.4

I investigated one provider in Florida and another in Las Vegas for billing for services that were said to have been provided at their main offices but the providers were actually out of the country during those time periods. In some investigations, I've been told that providers continued to bill for services while the providers were at conferences. As a fraud fighter, if you become aware of a time period(s) when a suspect provider was out of their office for extended days, make some notes about it and check to see if any services were claimed to have been provided on those dates. Remember to obtain proof from as many sources as possible to establish that the provider was actually not present during the time frame that services were reportedly provided.

In some cases, lesser educated healthcare personnel are required to be supervised when they provide services. This may be true when residents in the neurology or psychological care fields perform certain types of services. Many insurance companies and government programs allow those lesser educated personnel to perform services but they must be "supervised" by a more experienced provider. If there is only one supervising doctor at the facility and he/she is away on vacation, at a conference, or out of the country, there could be a whole lot of false claims involved.

Along these lines, sometimes supervising doctors' names appear on claim forms for more services than could possibly be provided or performed in any 24-hour period or any 1-week period.

WAR STORY 2.5

A resident neurologist once told me that his supervisor (a neurologist) was required to be present to supervise the resident doctors on the staff—especially during patient examinations. But the resident told me that the doctor was not present during examinations and just reviewed and signed patient charts. I empathized with the residents because they needed to pass their residencies to become licensed as neurologists, and the absent doctor was the one who was responsible for writing their evaluations. If the residents complained to their supervisor, they could suffer the consequences, which could negatively affect their careers.

It's important to remember that all the records and documents in the world usually won't prove your case. At some point you need witnesses. Remember that the potential witness's livelihood could be affected for telling the truth, so use tact when conducting such interviews.

Corruption: Kickbacks, bribery, and self-referrals—The Stark Law

Corruption might be described as an illegal act done (or intentionally not done when required to be) by a person with intent, which gives some advantage inconsistent with their official duty and the rights of others.

Most often, something of value is provided (directly or indirectly) in exchange for the act. Sometimes, the person performing the illegal act (or omission) personally benefits from their actions. The Stark Law (42 U.S.C. 1395nn) prohibits providers from making Medicare and Medicaid patient referrals to places or others in which they or their family members have a financial interest. (Please see other sources for legal definitions.)

Self-referrals remind me of a television comedy show in the 1960s in which one character acted as the small town's shopkeeper, justice of the peace, postmaster, and publisher of the town's newspaper. Sometimes, all he had to do was flip over the sign on his desk or put on a different hat to represent himself as filling a different capacity. In some schemes, the doctor is basically referring patients for examinations and tests at the same or other locations in which the doctor will also profit either by ownership, relatives' ownership, or by kickbacks or bribes. Keep in mind that kickbacks and bribes can be in many forms besides cash, checks, or money orders.

WAR STORY 2.6

During one investigation I conducted, a government contracting officer intentionally avoided obtaining required bid prices from different vendors before awarding small dollar purchase orders and instead awarded the orders to a favored vendor that was paying him bribes. The bribes included cash, cashier's checks, cars, and even payments for the contracting officer's daughter's wedding. The contracting officer also received free stays at the vendor's condo in Florida.

All expense paid vacations are actually a pretty common form of kickbacks. Gift cards and prepaid credit cards are also a sneaky way to disguise payments. Although many financial transactions can be completed electronically and by the Internet, do not rule out that gifts and gratuities could be shipped through a number of different carriers. Sometimes, finding legally obtained evidence of shipments (especially letter-sized envelopes) gets you closer to proving your case.

Double billing

Double billings are easier to detect because almost everyone uses computers to keep track of accounts payable and receivable. But some smaller entities are not as well organized as others. I know of one contractor who put extreme pressure on his accounts payable employee to pay all invoices as soon as they were received and falling behind was inexcusable. Little did that company owner know (or care) that many vendors were taking full advantage of this and submitting two and three invoices for the very same work—and receiving payment multiple times for each claim.

Durable medical equipment and supplier fraud

Durable medical equipment (DME) and other suppliers are capable of committing all kinds of different fraud schemes, some of which have already been mentioned. The most often talked about is the "scooter scheme," which involves powered wheelchairs. It has been reported that Medicare alone has paid billions of dollars for wheelchairs and scooters. Essentially, doctors can write prescriptions for scooters or powered wheeled chairs for those who are considered too weak to use a cane, walker, or nonpowered wheelchair. As a fraud fighter, you know that there should be a corresponding medical examination preceding such a prescription. If not, that is a pretty bright red flag.

The large-scale problems occur when schemers solicit people (potential patients) to receive scooters, and transport the patients to the doctor (who is participating in the scheme). An often totally unnecessary prescription is then written and the scooter billed for. Frequently, the "patient" receives a little kickback for their participation and can keep the scooter (even if they don't need it). Sometimes, real doctors are not even involved—the fraudsters instead just use the doctors' names and provider numbers to fill the prescriptions. Oftentimes, fraudsters use the names of dead doctors. In short, be on the lookout for false prescriptions too.

Similarly, other DME items are fraudulently billed for including oxygen tanks, orthopedic braces, electric nerve stimulation kits, and even prosthetic limbs. Although less profitable for fraudsters, the scheme can also involve billings for diabetes test strips. Ghost shipments (mentioned previously) and defective products can also be a profitable scam.

WAR STORY 2.7

One contractor I investigated provided orthopedic shoes to the government under contract. The orthopedic shoes were supposed to have the most super duper staples on earth to hold the material in place. Instead, the contractor just used a desk stapler. The same contractor reportedly manufactured bone screws but I found he had actually imported them from another country. That was in violation of the contract's "Buy American" clause.

Another scheme involves shipping more items than originally ordered and then billing for them. As previously mentioned, sometimes payers just assume that whatever is written on the invoice is correct so they pay it. Even if the payers physically check the inventory they will find that all of the items were received, so it is hard to conclude there was a fraud committed.

Although there may not be any perceived harm in it, some suppliers submit bills, get paid, and then ship. Essentially, they are receiving tax-free loans. At some point, those suppliers usually go "belly-up" because they are in such financial despair. The last orders are the ones that usually end up unfilled even though payments have been made.

Some medical items are rented by patients for short-term use. Examples include scooters, wheelchairs, and even wheelchair ramps and lift chairs. Fraud could occur when the items are returned by the patients but the supplier just keeps on billing as if the items are still being used by the same patients.

Key things to remember when investigating DME and supplier fraud is that there should be billed doctor visits that precede the use of the equipment and supplies. If the doctor's office is located a few states away from many of the patients, that would be a red flag. If the prescribing doctor was dead when the prescription was written, that would be a brighter red flag. If both the patient and the doctor were dead when the prescription was written, slap somebody a high five even if it is someone in the janitorial crew because you got a good case. But then you would also have to identify and locate the bad guys.

False cost reports

I strongly suggest that you have an accountant or auditor provide assistance when investigating false cost reports. Some hospitals and inpatient (and perhaps outpatient) facilities receive a portion of their reimbursement from government programs (e.g., Medicare) based on financial information they provide regarding other types of cost they incur including overhead, bad debts, depreciation of assets, operating staffs, surgical rooms, square footage, and so forth. Consideration for payment is also given to the geographical (cost of living) area where the clinic or hospital is located. Fraud occurs when the information provided is false.

WAR STORY 2.8

A partial hospitalization clinic I investigated submitted false cost reports to Medicare. In addition to other false expenses listed, they included the cost of rental furniture. It was learned that the owners of the medical clinic also owned a furniture rental company. Their clinic was the only customer the furniture company had. But the owners listed furniture rentals at triple the price so that the government would reimburse more.

The cost reports were submitted annually to the government. Therefore, many false cost report claims were identified. Note that criminal and civil statutes usually read that if any portion of the claim for reimbursement is false, then the entire dollar amount of the claim is considered false. This could allow for huge dollar prosecutions, judgments, and settlements. As previously stated, when investigating any type of fraud, if you identify one fraud scheme there might be other schemes too. This particular clinic committed just about all of the fraud schemes listed in this chapter. The investigation resulted in a multimillion dollar civil recovery.

False dates of service

False dates of service on insurance claim forms is a similar, and sometimes the same, scheme as billing for services not rendered. In these cases, you might find that a patient was seen by a doctor on one day, but the claims list services for two consecutive days. This could allow for two doctor visits to be (falsely) billed rather than just one visit. Another example could be simply billing for dates when no services were provided at all.

WAR STORY 2.9

While reviewing and analyzing one provider's claims history, I noticed that some billings were submitted for seeing the same patients several times a week for care that wouldn't warrant being seen that often. When reviewing the patient charts, I found there was no evidence that the patients were ever seen on most of those days billed for.

Another similar scheme occurs when the provider bills for services provided to many of the patient's other family members on the same days. A slight variation is after treating one patient for 30 days, they reportedly start treating other family members for 30 days after that. The time periods could be different. All of the services could be legitimate, but depending on the types of services provided, it could be a red flag. Sometimes, the other family members are never actually seen by the doctor.

Author's Note: *When reviewing claim dates to determine when services were supposedly provided, remember to focus your attention on the dates of service, not the dates the claims were signed or submitted. Sometimes, claims are not* *signed and submitted for several days after the reported service. And oftentimes, claims are resubmitted, and therefore, the dates on the claims may be several days or even months after the service(s) was provided.*

False location of service

The location of service is required to be listed when an insurance claim form is completed. Sometimes you'll find that the location listed is not accurate. When I perform my initial examinations and analysis of claim forms and patient records, I try to give the providers the benefit of the doubt until it's apparent that there is a pattern of fraud. In other words, if a provider wrote down the wrong location on one or just a couple claims, I chalk it off to human error. (Maybe I shouldn't.) But if I see a pattern of this, it must be further explored.

WAR STORY 2.10

During the investigation of an allergist, I reviewed patient records and claim forms that indicated patients were receiving allergy injections 4 or 5 days a week. I could not envision anyone stopping by the allergy clinic almost every day of the week for months at a time. That's just too darn inconvenient. When I interviewed some of the patients, they told me they didn't actually visit the allergy clinic to receive injections. Instead, they were handed stacks of filled syringes containing liquid antigens and then the patients later injected themselves at their own homes or elsewhere in the days that followed. Most of the patients said they enjoyed the convenience of not having to go to the allergy clinic to receive the injections.

But every single claim form I reviewed listed the location of service for each injection as being at the allergy clinic. I found it interesting that the days of the week listed were always weekdays and never weekends. The patients I interviewed said they sometimes injected themselves on weekends as well as weekdays. The patients also told me that they never injected themselves more than three times per week, not four or five times a week as the claim forms indicated. In short, the claims were false because the number of injections was inflated and the location of service was false. I suspected the reason the clinic never listed weekend dates for injections was because they knew it would be a red flag since it was known the clinic was closed on weekends.

The insurance companies and government programs reported that they never would have reimbursed any dollar amount for the claims had they known the injections were not given at the clinic.

It was those insurance companies and government programs' policies that the patients should be monitored for a few minutes after each injection to ensure they did not have a reaction to the antigens. That being said, almost every single claim submitted for reimbursement was considered false. (***Note:*** Some insurance plans may differ on this requirement.)

Incorrect reporting of diagnosis or procedures

An unscrupulous provider could intentionally list a more serious diagnosis than is warranted, which requires additional procedures to be performed (e.g., lab testing, examinations, and perhaps even hospitalization). Obviously, on a fee-for-services basis, this could be very profitable for the provider and others. I've often compared this scheme to the one used in the auto repair industry when a customer drives in for an oil change and once the car is on the rack, the customer is incorrectly told they need new brakes, a new air filter, new wiper blades, and so forth.

WAR STORY 2.11

The day before I wrote this page, I called my car service dealer and scheduled an oil change and tire rotation. Even though the technician was viewing my car's maintenance history on his computer screen, he kept trying to sell me the more expensive 30,000-mile full maintenance package. The problem was I already had that work completed 2 months before. I wondered why he wanted me to have it done again. (Actually, I knew why.)

Since I started to distrust the employees, I inconspicuously marked my car's two rear tires with chalk before bringing the car in for the oil change and tire rotation. I also photographed the car tires and chalk marks close up and from a distance. Well, they billed me for the oil change and tire rotation. They also told me I needed new windshield wipers and a new air filter. I gave them approval to change those too. But when I walked to my car after they were reportedly finished, I saw the chalk marks were still on the two rear tires. Since I also had the photos on my smartphone, I proved my point pretty quickly. I don't think I've been called "sir" so many times in 1 minute in my life after that. They took the car back and rotated the tires and gave me a complete refund on everything. Although I'm sure the wiper blades were changed, I wonder if they actually changed the air filter and oil.

As implied from this, it is also possible that the providers bill for things they never did or supplies or medication that was never given. Patients often complain that hospitals bill for items they never received. Although it's not considered fraud, hospital costs for even things like aspirin can be astronomical. For example, for two acetaminophen tablets some hospitals charge the same price that a customer could buy an entire bottle full at local drug store. That's just the tip of the iceberg.

A fraud fighter could look for a pattern where a patient is discharged from a hospital just before his/her insurance would lapse and then readmitted soon after for a different procedure. I'll emphasize again that you'd be looking for the pattern of such occurrences as that would be more indicative of fraud. Another example of incorrect reporting of procedures is a scheme called "unbundling," which is separately listed later in this chapter.

Lab fraud

Labs often play large roles in healthcare, and sometimes physicians might order unnecessary lab work if they have a financial interest in the lab or receive kickbacks for the services. Hospitals might increase their profits by ordering lab work. The independent clinical labs need work (patients) to make a profit. Therefore, they need to be known by the physicians and hospitals. As an incentive to use their lab, unscrupulous lab owners might offer kickbacks to those who provide referrals.

In addition, labs might be able to persuade physicians to request specific tests on a routine basis (whether needed or not). The labs also submit their own claims for payment to insurance companies and government programs for their services. Therefore, it is possible that in addition, physicians and hospitals labs can also bill for tests never performed and for patients never actually seen. Once again, if lab work was billed, there should ordinarily be a doctor or hospital visit preceding it.

Another type of lab is a Rolling Lab. They are often contained in semitrailers. You've probably seen them parked at shopping centers or elsewhere. Some labs rent temporary office space or use other's space for short-term periods. They often seek and solicit individuals (particularly low income and the elderly) to have physical examinations performed at absolutely no cost to the patient. As you know, once the lab has the patients' names, dates of birth, and Social Security Numbers (often referred to as Protected Identifying Information), they can do a lot of billing to Medicaid and Medicare or other insurance companies. Some labs have been known to offer individuals incentives (gifts) for participating in the exams. The sky is the limit as to the number of claims that can be submitted. Investigators might find it extremely difficult to locate some of those individual patients because they may have no permanent address or telephone number.

Misrepresenting a patient's name

Factually, in order to submit a healthcare insurance claim for payment, certain information about a patient is needed. That information typically includes a patient's name, sex, date of birth, and Social Security Number. If the listed patient is different from the beneficiary (for example a child or spouse of the actual policyholder) then the beneficiary's information is also needed.

Author's Note: *It's worth noting that organized crime, hackers, and other crime rings have been known to obtain patients' Protected Identifying Information to submit massive amounts of false claims. Sometimes, uninsured patients "borrow," or obtain others' identification cards and falsely list others' names to receive care at no or less cost.*

A scheming provider may list the names of patients that were never actually seen. Even the names of deceased individuals have been known to be used by providers to get reimbursement.

The listing of other family members of patients that were actually seen is a common example of misrepresenting the name of patient or recipient of services. In short, do not always assume that just because a patient's name is listed on claim forms that they actually were seen or received services.

In recent years, several insurance carriers and government healthcare program organizations were found to have failed to adequately safeguard the Protected Identifying Information of insurance beneficiaries, and the information was obtained by hackers or others. Some beneficiary information was contained in employees' laptop computers that were reported missing or stolen. As stated, Protected Identifying Information can be extremely valuable to fraudsters who submit false billings for payment.

Misrepresenting the name of the provider

Insurance companies and government programs base their reimbursement decisions on information listed on the submitted claim forms. Factually, in some cases lesser educated healthcare personnel often provide services on patients. It may be permissible for a provider (for example, a physician) to supervise those lesser educated providers or assistants and still list the higher educated person as the provider. The definition of *supervision* may vary; some say that the provider must at least be in the building where the service was provided.

But sometimes the insurance companies allow lesser educated and approved healthcare providers to provide services and list their own names on the claim forms. The insurance companies sometimes reimburse those lesser educated personnel at a lower rate than higher educated personnel.

By falsely listing the higher educated person as the provider, the insurance company or government program may be deceived and pay more.

WAR STORY 2.12

When investigating a psychological care facility, I learned that most of the providers at that facility were lesser educated than doctors. Some were licensed clinical social workers, some were pastoral counselors, and some were not even licensed by their state to provide such services. The insurance company's policy was to pay less when lesser educated licensed providers performed the services. But a doctor signed 100 percent of their claim forms. I learned that the doctor only worked at the facility 2 days a week. When I interviewed the doctor and inquired why he signed all the claim forms, he said with confidence that he was permitted to do so because he was the supervising physician. He said he came in twice a week and reviewed the patient files. I asked the doctor if he knew that some of the psychological care providers were not licensed, and he responded, "Well then why the hell are they working here?" He assumed that the owners only hired licensed providers. The doctor then said to me, "I guess I'm the goat." I responded, "Not if you testify!"

As stated in the section, "Billing When Provider Is Out of the Office," sometimes residents are permitted to examine patients and perform other services when "supervised" by a physician. But sometimes the physician actually plays little or no part in the supervision, yet the supervisor's name appears on the claim forms. When investigating such instances, the patient chart entries (completed by the actual providers) can be of great value to proving who actually provided the services. However, you should anticipate the supervising physician's defense will be that they "supervised." In these types of instances, it would be great to also have witnesses who can provide firsthand accounts of what role the supervisor(s) actually played in the services provided.

Author's Note: *It's not that unusual to learn when conducting interviews that the residents or others may have kept their own copies of records and charts to keep themselves out of trouble. Sometimes they take those records home and store them.*

Prescription drug fraud

Prescription drug fraud is recognized as a nationwide problem. Prescription drug abuse might even be considered an epidemic. One reason for this is because some of the drugs are so addictive and another is because the street value of some of the drugs (particularly painkillers) is outrageous—up to 10 times the purchase price. These two reasons alone contribute greatly to the causes of prescription drug fraud.

Pharmacists and their staffs have access to all types of prescription drugs. Strict inventory procedures ordinarily provide accountability. But a false or fabricated paper trail can permit controlled drugs to be dispersed or removed with less detection.

Some physicians and others who are licensed to write prescriptions for drugs are also known to be involved in prescription drug fraud schemes. Patients are also known to go to several different doctors (*doctor shopping*) to obtain the prescription drugs they want even when not needed.

Listed here are some of the schemes known to be used by providers (including pharmacists or their staff):

- *False or unnecessary issuance of prescription drugs*: Some doctors have been known to not only write unnecessary prescriptions for patients that visit their office but actually write prescriptions "on the street" for a profit.
- *Kickbacks*: Some doctors and others who write prescriptions accept kickbacks from others as an incentive to prescribe "their drugs." There is an obvious danger in this as one can suspect that prescriptions may be written for people who don't even need them. It's also not fair to the drug company competitors who operate legitimately.
- *Partial filling of prescriptions*: Some pharmacies have been known to partially fill prescription orders, bill for the entire amount and then instruct the patient to return later to obtain the rest of the pills. Very often, the patients never return for the other pills, so the pharmacy profits for billing for prescription drugs never provided.
- *Billing for brand name drugs but providing generic*: Some pharmacies have been found to bill insurance companies or patients for brand name drugs but actually provide patients with less expensive generic drugs.
- *Counterfeit products*: Providing counterfeit, watered-down, and lesser-quality prescriptions is also a profitable fraud scheme. Some medications (especially cancer drugs) are extremely expensive. Providing lesser ingredients can result in higher (illegal) profits.
- *Billing for larger quantities/packages*: This scheme is also pretty simple where pharmacies prescribed the patient with less quantity than prescribed. How many of us actually count the number of pills contained in a prescription bottle as soon as we open it? Most won't realize a shortage until days or weeks later and will lose any argument because of the time delay before complaining.

- *False beneficiary billings for drugs never provided*: In addition to having access to prescription drugs, pharmacies, and their staffs also have access to patient and beneficiary Protected Identifying Information along with their corresponding healthcare insurance or government program insurance coverage policy numbers. A bad apple with access to all that information can do a lot of damage. This scheme involves claims submitted by the pharmacy to insurance companies for prescription drugs reportedly dispensed to beneficiaries whose Protected Identifying Information was used, which was obtained from the pharmacy's computerized historic dispensing records. These could be simple false claims in which no drugs were actually removed from the shelf or when actually removing the equivalent drugs from the pharmacy's inventory and getting the beneficiaries' insurance companies to pay for the drugs.

WAR STORY 2.13

A pharmacist I investigated in Las Vegas, Nevada, obtained patient beneficiary information and their corresponding insurance company information from his pharmacy's computer database. Next, he submitted numerous insurance claims for small quantities of painkillers under each beneficiary's name. He even made cash co-payments into the pharmacy's cash drawer so that the pharmacy wouldn't detect a financial shortage. Then he stole the equivalent number of painkillers off the shelf and sold them on the street for 10 times the store sale price. His scheme would have worked even longer had he been smart enough to also fabricate written prescriptions which were required to be maintained at the pharmacy. In fact, the only reason he got caught was because an audit found that he dispensed too many pills without first having doctor prescriptions. I'm sure somewhere he silently said to himself, "Oops!" He later confessed and was sentenced to prison.

- *Buybacks*: Some pharmacies have been known to actually buy back prescription drugs from patients. They often purchase them back at a discount and resell them at a higher price.
- *Shell pharmacies*: Sometimes, ownership is hidden so that the real owners are not known, and some pharmacies don't exist at all and have temporary addresses to submit bogus prescription drug claims.
- *Illegal online pharmacies*: Recent publicity has shown that there are many national and international online pharmacies that illegally ship controlled substances (especially painkillers) to individuals

without prescriptions. Some overnight delivery service companies have even been the subject of recent federal government investigations for allegedly knowingly transporting the improper shipments. The Department of Justice also pursued an Internet search engine service provider for profiting from ads purchased from online pharmacies that were improperly selling prescription drugs.

Unbundling

As previously stated, unbundling is similar to and perhaps the same as the section, "Incorrect Reporting of Diagnosis or Procedures." Unbundling is sometimes also called fragmentation or exploding. This scheme is essentially billing for two or more services separately that should be included in a single package coding. I have often compared unbundling to going to a fast food restaurant and ordering a value meal and after paying you look at the receipt and find they charged you for each item separately (burger, fries, and soda) causing you to pay more than if they rang it up as the advertised value meal.

Some describe unbundling as billing for a comprehensive code and also billing for the component codes. Either way, this scheme involves listing two or more individual codes separately in a claim to get reimbursed more money for doing the same exact work (providing the same exact service), which should have been included in a single code. One example of unbundling might be when blood test panels are tested by laboratories but instead of billing this under one code (like they are supposed to), they list each test (code) separately resulting in higher payments. Some healthcare providers seeking to increase profits will unbundle tests or procedures (including surgery) and bill separately for each component of the group, which totals more expensively than the special reimbursement rate.

Upcoding

Upcoding is essentially a fraud scheme where the healthcare provider provides a service but lists a similar code that pays a higher reimbursement. An example of this might be a doctor that treats a patient for a hairline fracture and tells the patient to stay off their feet as much as possible but they bill as if they put on a cast. (Unrelated, they might also later bill for removing the cast, which would be billing for services not provided.)

Wave treatment

This scheme traditionally takes place in hospitals during inpatient care where a doctor comes in and only sees the patient momentarily but bills for 15- or 30-minute increments of time. Some reports include a doctor walking the hospital halls first thing in the morning and waving "hello" to their patients and billing as if services were provided. A subcategory of this might be "gang visits" in which doctors visit nursing homes and charges for 15 or more nursing home visits without actually providing any individual services.

Waiving deductibles or co-payments

Recently, there have been many changes in the options individuals have to obtain healthcare insurance coverage and the amounts (if any) beneficiaries pay for healthcare. But many insurance companies and government programs require beneficiaries to pay a designated dollar amount as a co-payment each time they visit a healthcare facility. Some plans may also require the beneficiary to first pay a deductible dollar amount before insurance pays any or certain costs. Part of the rationale behind deductibles and co-payments may be that if beneficiaries must first pay something when they visit the doctor perhaps they won't make unnecessary visits and therefore keep the overall healthcare costs down.

Some providers have been known to illegally waive those required costs for their patients. Some providers argue that they only waive co-payments for the patient who cannot afford to pay them. However, waiving those costs defeats the purpose of the arrangement. It also encourages patients to keep coming back to that doctor or facility—perhaps unnecessarily and it certainly puts other doctors that play by the rules at a disadvantage. It's theorized that the provider is recapturing those waived costs somewhere otherwise they'd be losing money and therefore, the insurance company or program can potentially be suffering the losses.

The bottom line is if the insurance policy or program requires co-payments to be made by those patients, then the co-payments cannot be waived by the provider.

Author's Note: *If conducting a criminal or civil investigation into such a scheme, it can be helpful to learn if the provider previously signed a document(s) agreeing to abide by that insurance company or program's billing policies and procedures. If it can be proven that the provider understood and agreed to the billing rules and then elected not to follow them, your case will be quite a bit stronger.*

The fraud schemes listed earlier are those committed by the scheming providers that participate in "fee-for-services" programs for reimbursement. That simply means that they are paid for every service they provide and bill for. However, worth mentioning is a scheme that occurs when providers are paid a certain dollar amount per year for each patient, or when patients' insurance policies have "caps" on the reimbursable dollar amounts for care. In those cases, a patient may not receive all the care they should because the provider won't get paid more for doing more. There are times when the patient will suddenly be considered "well" once the cap for coverage is met. In other words, the patient is told to go home because "they are healed" once the reimbursable dollar limit is met. But then the patient returns for more care once the new policy year begins.

Some suggest that hospitals should be financially penalized if patients are readmitted too soon after being discharged. My concern is that if hospitals are penalized for readmissions, they may choose not to readmit people that should be readmitted or delay the readmission just to avoid the penalty.

Although not a *scheme* per se, it is worth noting that many hospitals and perhaps others are known to have "charity" and "bad debt" write-offs, which no doubt benefits them for tax and promotional purposes. But it should be noted that the dollar amounts listed for those "write-offs" are most probably determined by their listed full (nondiscounted) "charge master" prices, which are not the same prices that insurance companies and government programs actually pay. The providers might say they provided millions or thousands of dollars in charity services, but that's based on their own made-up nondiscounted dollar figures.

For example, a hospital might report that their normal master price charge for a Code 123 Service is $1000.00. But factually, Medicare might pay $120.00 for that same service; they might charge discounted insurance companies $550.00 for it; and they might charge people without insurance $1000.00. Therefore, their annual "charity write-off" could be *huge*! And the amount they charge the uninsured is just as huge. But sometimes they will negotiate with a noncovered patient to only pay a lesser cost. So, is the $1000 their real charge?—maybe or maybe not.

Author's Note: *One doctor told me that nonprofit hospitals are required to discount and/or waive the cost of uninsured indigent and/or low income patients to maintain the hospital's nonprofit tax status.*

Common provider fraud red flags

As a fraud fighter, it's smart to know the red flags that indicate when provider fraud may have occurred or is occurring. To make this a little more entertaining, I will provide this information in comedian Jeff Foxworthy fashion by giving this topic the subheading:

You might be a healthcare fraud provider if

- You are providing more services than could possibly have been completed in the time period billed for
- You bill for services that you are not trained to provide (e.g., you are a chiropractor and you are billing for surgery)

- You have a sudden increase in the number of billings for a particular type of service
- You have a sudden increase in total patient billings
- Your eyes show dollar signs when you are scheduled to provide group therapy
- All of your patients' family members are being treated for the same exact conditions
- Your patients suddenly "get well" once their annual insurance cap is met
- Many of your patients home addresses are very distant from your office (especially in faraway states)
- Many of your patients' addresses are the same as yours or your employees
- Many of your patients share the same mailing address
- Your business address is not what it purports to be (like it's a liquor store)
- Some of the patients that you claim you are treating are actually deceased
- You submit insurance claim forms listing one or more providers of care who you know are deceased
- You bill for patients' ambulance services but the patients are never seen by doctors after they arrive
- You bill for surgery but not for an exam before the surgery
- You consider "unbundling" as your idea of being detailed
- You intentionally talk very slowly and often repeat yourself while watching the clock during counseling sessions
- All of your patients have blood drawn for lab testing (but you don't work in a lab)
- You bill for dispensing prescriptions to patients who never saw a doctor first
- Many of your patients and their relatives are prescribed the same drugs (especially painkillers)
- You bill as if you dispensed expensive cancer drugs but the patients were never diagnosed with cancer
- You bill for services provided on Sundays and federal holidays when your facility is closed on those days
- The dates on your dictation notes regularly differ from the service dates you billed for
- You bill for patient visits at your facility but the patients never set foot in your facility
- You bill for patient services but there are no notes in the patient files indicating the patients were seen, and your appointment book has no record of the patients scheduled for visits

- Hospitals and others keep complaining that your shipments are short
- Hospitals and others keep complaining that you deliver the wrong items
- Insurance companies and government programs complain that you frequently double bill
- You constantly call insurance companies and government programs requesting quick payment
- You "wave" to more patients than you actually treat—and bill for it
- You prescribe wheelchairs to all of your patients who are on Medicare
- You own another company that leases office furniture or medical equipment to your own medical practice (at inflated prices)
- You bill for services you provided at your office while you are actually out of state on vacations or at conventions
- Your suppliers or other entities keep sending you money, gifts, and pay for your vacations
- You inflate more cost report expenses than you do surgical gloves to give to kids

The next chapter goes beyond the providers and describes others who commit healthcare fraud and some of their schemes.

chapter three

Other healthcare fraudsters and schemes

So, who else besides providers commit healthcare fraud? Just about anyone within the healthcare, insurance, government program, or claims systems, and anyone outside those systems is capable of committing healthcare fraud. However, it's been my experience that as a group (with the exception of perhaps organized crime and hackers), most of the other fraudsters cause less total dollar losses than providers.

Others that commit healthcare fraud

Others that commit healthcare fraud include but are not limited to the following:

- Patients and insurance beneficiaries
- Employers
- Insurance company employees and government insurance program employees
- Third-party administrators and fiscal intermediaries
- Fake business entities
- Telephone and telemarketing scammers
- Hackers
- Organized crime

Perhaps a better question is, "Is there any group that is not known to commit healthcare fraud?" My instinctive response would be, "Yes, dead people don't commit healthcare fraud." But it's been proven all too often that the names of deceased providers and patients have been used to commit healthcare fraud—so I guess no groups are exempt.

The following sections discuss others that commit healthcare fraud along with some of their schemes.

Patients and beneficiaries that commit healthcare fraud

- *Doctor shopping*: Doctor shopping is when a patient goes to two or more doctors to receive the same or other controlled medication for which they don't have an actual medical need. This scheme is often committed by patients to obtain prescription drugs (often painkillers) for personal use or to sell on the street for a profit.
- *Prescription drug pad thefts*: Some patients (as well as employees of medical facilities) steal prescription drug pads and then write their own prescriptions and forge the provider's name on them in order to obtain prescription drugs either for personal use, to share with others, or to sell on the street. Some patients have also been known to alter legitimate handwritten paper prescriptions by adding the quantities or the number of authorized refills.
- *Lending insurance cards*: Some patients who have insurance have been known to lend their insurance cards (and perhaps along with their own identification cards) to others (especially friends) that do not have insurance coverage. This allows the person holding the insurance card to (illegally) receive healthcare at no or little costs. Some lenders may also charge the users a fee for providing their insurance card and information.
- *False dependents*: Some parents who have "family" healthcare insurance coverage have been known to falsely list as dependents of others who are not actually their dependents in order to (illegally) cover others with insurance they would not otherwise have. Prior to 2015 and the implementation of the Affordable Care Act, the annual premium costs for "family coverage" was most often the same whether the policyholder had two or more dependents. But since then, many employers charge their employees more to include their spouses and/or dependents.
- *Stolen identification*: Hackers, organized crime rings, and others have been known to illegally obtain insurance beneficiary and patient information and then sell or use the information to commit various types of fraud—including healthcare fraud. Fraudsters can also create or obtain fake identification cards and fake insurance cards, which match legitimate beneficiary and patient names and information to obtain healthcare coverage and commit other frauds or crimes.
- *In furtherance of other insurance fraud schemes*: Employees have been known to fake on-the-job injuries in order to collect workers' compensation. Some employees are actually injured elsewhere but report they were injured on the job. To further their scheme, they will need to see a doctor to have the injury documented. The first

scenario results in totally unnecessary medical examinations and perhaps treatment, and both scenarios result in the employer or the employers' insurance company paying for examinations and treatment, which they should not have paid.

Another example is when fraudsters stage traffic accidents or other accidents (like slips and falls) in order to later sue insurance companies, businesses, and individuals. Those fraudsters may not have been injured at all, but they claim they were while hoping to receive out-of-court settlements or other payments that they do not deserve. It should be noted that sometimes healthcare providers and the fraudsters' attorneys actually conspire with the fraudsters and also profit from the scheme.

Both of the schemes not only result in dollar losses from the unnecessary examinations and possible care but also cause or contribute to the increases in healthcare insurance premiums.

- *Busing patients*: Some larger-scale fraudsters approach indigent people, drug addicts, and others who are less stable that have Medicaid coverage and pay them small dollar amounts (*or booze and cigarettes*) either to provide their personal identifying information (so the fraudsters can later submit false claims) or to actually be examined or receive examinations or care that they don't actually need. Some people living on the streets or in temporary shelters are desperate for any form of compensation and will gladly participate if they can make a few bucks. Sometimes, the fraudsters even load the individuals onto a bus or van and drive them to the medical clinics (or store fronts) that are also in the scheme.

Employers that commit healthcare fraud

- *Misclassification of employee job functions*: Employers that purchase healthcare and liability insurance for their employees must pay annual premiums based on the information they provide to their insurance company. The insurance company bases their price on the number of employees, potential risk, and other factors. Some employers have been known to misclassify the types of work some employees perform in order to give the appearance that there is less risk. For example, an office clerk has a less risk of receiving injury than a skyscraper window washer.

  When the employer intentionally provides inaccurate or misleading information to their insurance company for the purpose of paying less for insurance—that's fraud.
- *False reporting the number of employees*: Some employers list the names of family members and friends as if being employed by the company when they are not actually employed there. This allows the

employer to claim the cost of those friends and family members as a business expense and allows the friends and family members to have insurance coverage that they are not actually entitled to.

- *Underreporting injuries*: Because an employer's insurance premiums might increase if claims are made for on-the-job injuries, some employers have been known not to report all injuries to their insurance companies and instead pay for an injured employee's care and treatment out of pocket. I know of one entity that received bonuses from the government for not having any work-related injuries. But in reality, some employees were injured and sitting at home collecting their pay (under the table).
- *False claims*: Employers are also in a position to submit employee healthcare claims to insurance companies. As such, this allows the opportunity for claims to be altered, falsified, or costs inflated.

  Self-insured employers can also alter and falsely increase the costs incurred for employee healthcare services and treatment or completely fabricate costs incurred for employee care and list the inflated cost as a business expense to decrease their tax liability.

Insurance company and government insurance program employees

- *Embezzlement and dummy accounts*: There are numerous ways that employees who work for healthcare insurance companies and government insurance programs can commit fraud. Factually, they have access to all of their policyholder and dependents' Protected Identifying Information as well as information about providers. That information can easily be stolen and shared or sold to others or put to personal use in a variety of different fraud schemes.

Just as we often read about bookkeepers who embezzle money by writing checks to themselves and skimming funds, anyone with access to volumes of patient and provider information as well as the claim submission process could rake in huge amounts of dollars illegally.

The list of potential schemes is almost endless. Dummy accounts can be created to receive payments as well as real patients' addresses changed. For example, if a bunch of insurance beneficiaries with different last names were found to have the same addresses as an insurance company employee or government insurance program employee, that would be an obvious red flag.

It would be difficult to detect if an employee was stealing patient's Protected Identifying Information or provider information and selling it. Fortunately, we don't read about these types of occurrences very often but I'm not sure that if an employee was found to be committing such frauds that the employers would want such information made public. At some point, you just have to trust someone. Truth be told; during my professional career, I've never had occasion to question the integrity of any employees in the private or public healthcare insurance industry.

Third-party administrators and fiscal intermediaries

Many healthcare providers actually subcontract out their insurance claims process. Some insurance companies and government programs also outsource their claims processing. Because of this, employees of third-party administrators and fiscal intermediaries have the same opportunities to commit fraud as described earlier for the employees of healthcare insurance companies and government insurance programs. One might speculate that because those employees don't work directly for those insurance companies or government programs, that some might not be quite as concerned if the insurance companies or government programs lose money. During my career, I've never had occasion to question the integrity of any employees of third-party administrators or fiscal intermediaries.

- *Sub-of-the-subscammers*: Although not just applicable to third-party administrators and fiscal intermediaries, whenever information and data are released to or made available to any other subcontractors, there is an opportunity for a security breach. Factually, some entities outsource their scanning and optical character recognition (OCR), which converts images of typewritten or printed text into machine-coded text so that the information can be edited, searched, stored, and displayed. *Heck, when you come right down to it, even the janitorial crew can sometimes gain access to information that they should not be able to.*

Fake business entities

- *Shell companies, storefronts, and mailbox rentals*: Once patients' Protected Identifying Information is obtained illegally, there is no limit to the amount of fraud that can occur. Numerous cases have been identified and prosecuted in which fraudsters opened shell companies and storefronts and rented post office (P.O.) boxes or commercial mailboxes to further their misdeeds (and receive illegal payments) for short-term periods. All too often, false claims are submitted to many different insurance companies and government insurance programs, and not long after payments are received, the fraudsters have fled or moved along.

Some storefronts actually have patients come in for services and examinations, and once their Protected Identifying Information is obtained, the fraudsters submitted inflated and/or false claims in for reimbursement. Sometimes, people covered by Medicare or Medicaid that are not doing well financially are enticed to provide their Protected Identifying Information and/or participate in exams or treatment by giving them small freebies.

Telephone and telemarketing scammers

Telephone and telemarketing scammers are also responsible for large amounts of healthcare fraud—especially against Medicare. Some scammers make cold calls trying to identify Medicare recipients and then convince them to provide their Medicare numbers by offering things like tropical pain creams to relieve their chronic pain. Sometimes, doctors, pharmacist, and suppliers conspire in the scam.

We've all seen more than our share of television commercials advertising products exclusively for Medicare recipients for which the beneficiary may not have to pay any out of pocket expenses. Some of the scams include selling arthritis kits, which include various inexpensive braces and wraps for knees, ankles, and wrists, but sometimes, Medicare is billed for the more expensive higher-quality splints and braces.

Telephone scammers often persuade people (especially the elderly) to provide their Protected Identifying Information (including their Medicare numbers) resulting in later false or inflated billings to their insurance companies or government programs as well as other stolen identification crimes.

Author's Note: *Although people have been warned for years not to carry their Social Security card with them to prevent identity theft, at the time of this writing, Medicare cards do have individuals' Social Security Numbers embedded in them. The Social Security Numbers serve as unique patient identifiers and proof of insurance. The Department of Veterans Affairs and the Department of Defense reportedly implemented efforts years ago to replace members' Social Security Numbers with other unique identifiers; however, many of their previously issued identification or insurance cards are still being used that have the Social Security Number embedded or printed on them. In April 2015, President Obama signed a bill to eliminate the listing of people's Social Security Numbers on Medicare cards. The bill gave the Department of Health and Human Services 4 years to modernize cards for new beneficiaries and up to 4 additional years to replace cards previously issued to existing Medicare recipients. The expense of this change was or is estimated in the millions of dollars. Still, individuals will have to avoid unnecessarily providing their unique identifying information to others—especially to telephone and telemarketing scammers and other fraudsters.*

Hackers

- *Unlawful accessing and retrieval of electronically stored Protected Identifying Information*: Computer hackers have been proven to be extremely dangerous to all private and public industries. They search for and exploit the weaknesses in computer systems and networks. Subject to attack are the computer systems and networks of all healthcare providers, clinics, facilities (including hospitals), as well as all healthcare insurance companies, state-sponsored health insurance exchanges, government health insurance programs, third-party administrators and fiscal intermediaries, and so forth. Although some hackers perform their misdeeds just for enjoyment or overcoming the challenge, others retrieve and sell or use the information to commit various types of fraud.

It would not be surprising to learn that if and when any of these entities had their computer systems or networks illegally accessed, it might be kept low key and handled in-house because the potential backlash could affect some profits—including lowering of their stock prices and/or result in a decrease in the number of future customers or patients. That being said, although we have every right to be alarmed and troubled when informed about such breaches, we should be glad when we are alerted after such incidents so that defensive action can be initiated.

On a lesser scale, it has been reported that some scammers search through individuals' and company trash cans (termed "dumpster diving") to obtain individuals' Protected Identifying Information and some telephone-soliciting scammers pursue the same information over the phone to further their schemes. There are also numerous computer scams out there that solicit unsuspecting individuals to provide their personal information (e.g., computer phishing).

Organized crime

- *High-dollar fraud using Protected Identifying Information*: Organized crime within and outside of the United States has been responsible for millions or billions of dollars in healthcare fraud. As you know, Protected Identifying Information can be obtained electronically from anywhere on the globe—and often is. The schemes utilized are essentially the same as many described earlier. But it always comes down to submitting and receiving payments for false claims. Organized crime does this on the largest of scales. Although American federal investigative agencies work closely with law enforcement agencies in foreign countries, many culprits who were outside of the United States when their crimes were committed (or fled the United States after being detected or indicted) have yet to be held accountable for their criminal activity. Some street gangs in America also participate in these types of offenses.

Author's Note: *The Health and Human Services, Office of Inspector General's (OIG) website has a listing of the "OIG's Most Wanted Fugitives" who are wanted for defrauding Medicare and Medicaid. Over 100 are listed and include full-color photographs of the wanted personnel along with their background information as well as descriptions of their wrongdoings and the investigative case facts. There is also a similar listing and descriptions about captured fugitives. Healthcare fraud fighters are encouraged to visit the OIG's website to learn about these fraudsters and to obtain more details about the types of schemes, which have already been committed. For additional information, visit: http://oig.hhs.gov/fraud/fugitives/index.asp.*

Common healthcare fraudster red flags

As a fraud fighter, it is smart to know the red flags that indicate when fraud may have occurred or is occurring. As in the previous chapter, I'll provide this information in comedian Jeff Foxworthy fashion by giving this topic a subheading of

You might be a healthcare fraudster if

- Your insurance policy indicates you have more dependents than can fit into a Starbucks coffee shop
- You hope people crash into your automobile while you are driving
- You ask your doctor if you can have some blank prescription pads because your kids need scratch paper to color on
- Almost everyone in your neighborhood uses your name and insurance coverage whenever they need healthcare
- The laminated plastic on the ID card that you showed when checking in for healthcare is hotter than the cigarette in your mouth
- You hop on a bus to get examined by a doctor just because the driver offered you $25 bucks
- You drive a bus full of people to get examined by a doctor just because someone offered you $25 bucks
- You own a P.O. box or commercial mailbox rental that receives check payments from healthcare insurance companies and government programs, but you are not in any way associated with the healthcare profession
- You own your own company that provides physical manual labor, but your healthcare insurance application reflects most of your employees are office workers

- You have signs posted inside your business that reflect you haven't had any worksite injuries in over a year but some of your employees were recently driven home in ambulances after falling off the docks
- You work in the accounts receivable and payable department making a moderate salary yet you drive a fancy sports car, frequently travel to exotic places, and eat only at the finest restaurants
- People keep asking you if you have any more names to sell
- You tell people not to worry about phishing scams because they do not go fishing much anyways
- People keep chasing you away just because you rummage through their trash cans looking for papers
- Your temporary business door has names with "Doctor" in front of them, but nobody inside even has a high school diploma
- Your business associates often make you "an offer you cannot refuse" just to submit health insurance claim forms using all kinds of different addresses
- You think "Black Friday" is the best time to go "Dr. Shopping"

Summary

Now that you are knowledgeable about many of the healthcare fraudsters and their schemes, you are probably eager to put all of your knowledge and perhaps your other training and experience to work to deter, detect, and investigate instances of healthcare fraud. Just keep in mind that healthcare providers and everyone else are innocent until proven guilty. Sometimes, what appears to be criminal wrongdoing is actually just the result of poor policies and/or procedures and occasional mistakes. Don't try to send everyone to jail just because of couple administrative errors.

On the other hand, "Where there's smoke, there's fire." In my opinion, if you do find evidence of fraud, odds are that those wrongdoers repeatedly committed the same type of fraud (and other types of fraud and related acts) in the past and they've probably done so for a long time. In addition, many of the fraudsters you investigate know others who are engaged in similar schemes or are involved with others who are engaged in the same type or some other fraud (or have engaged in it in the past). If you are like me, you will be just as willing to investigate fraud whether it happened previously or is still ongoing.

The next chapter begins the process of learning how to successfully conduct healthcare fraud investigations. It provides an overview about healthcare fraud victims, investigators, complainants, laws, and statutes.

chapter four

Victims, investigators, complainants, laws, and statutes

Victims

The victims of healthcare fraud are many. Any insurance company, government program (federal, state, and municipal), employer (public and private), patient, policyholder, or other that actually paid for a fraudulent healthcare billing is a victim. Because healthcare fraud results in unjust payments, it directly or indirectly affects the dollar amounts paid for annual premiums, deductibles, co-payments, and other out-of-pocket healthcare expenses. Taxpayers are also impacted by healthcare fraud because money lost could have remained in their own pockets and/or put to better use.

While investigating healthcare fraud (especially provider fraud and organized crime), keep in mind that each separate investigation may actually have more than one financial victim because (in most cases) all patients are not insured by the same insurance companies or programs. Because most healthcare providers submit insurance claim forms to several different entities or programs for payment, be conscious of the fact that many different entities (and perhaps individuals) may have been victimized for the same violations that you are investigating.

Although each insurance company or program has its own policies and procedures, they can all be victimized by all or most of the schemes previously described. An example of an exception might be when one or more insurance companies do not require beneficiaries to make co-payments, while others do. Therefore, waiving co-payments may be a violation of one's policy but not another's.

Author's Note: *Don't assume that the rules, policies, and procedures for one insurance company or government program apply to all others. Inquire separately with each organization. If they have a pertinent written policy regarding the issue, ask for a copy of it and ascertain when it was implemented. Also obtain copies of any revisions and/or updates.*

Investigators of healthcare fraud

At some point, you'll have to decide if and when you will notify other potential victim insurance companies or government insurance programs about the apparent wrongdoing and your investigation. If you are going to notify other potential victim entities about your investigation, you should do so early because it will probably take them just as long as it took you (perhaps longer) to obtain provider information, claims histories, and other information they need just to consider or initiate their investigation(s).

Beware that other insurance companies or programs may have already initiated an investigation(s) regarding the same suspect(s), perhaps for the same wrongdoing, and you might jeopardize each other's cases if you don't communicate with each other. If you are working jointly, you should be able to plan and implement your investigative strategy together such that it works to everyone's advantage and makes the best use of resources and time.

WAR STORY 4.1

While working as a federal agent for the Department of Defense (DoD), I was notified that a healthcare provider may have defrauded TRICARE (the active and retired military's health insurance program). After reviewing the allegations and claims history, I notified several other federal investigative agencies that also investigated healthcare fraud to determine if their programs paid the suspect significant funds for the service codes in question. A federal criminal investigator from the Health and Human Services and Office of Inspector General (HHS-OIG) who was responsible for investigating Medicare fraud provided an affirmative response.

As a result, we conducted a joint investigation that identified significant dollar losses to both TRICARE and Medicare. We also teamed on many interviews of patients that had insurance coverage by both Medicare and TRICARE and when conducting interviews of current and former employees of the healthcare-providing facility. Since we alternated writing the summary interview reports, we also saved time. The case had more appeal to the criminal and civil prosecutors because there were two victim agencies and the identified dollar loss was higher.

On a negative note, several months after my initial query to other federal investigative agencies, a federal agent from another agency "popped up" and said their agency was also impacted by the fraud. Since our investigation was almost complete, that agent's unexpected arrival delayed prosecution considerations. In essence, the new agent unjustly benefitted for our already accomplished hard work. We later learned that a particular agent had a historic reputation for their late participation on many other joint cases and later taking credit for other agents' already completed work.

The term federal agents have for that agent's actions is called "coattailing." It is when agents or investigators open joint cases, but one agent (or agency) fails to contribute to the investigative effort yet they claim credit for the indictments, convictions, judgments, and dollar recoveries. Factually, some of the best-known and respected investigative agents and agencies are notorious for coattailing. These agents often receive awards and promotions, and their agencies' annual budgets are increased because it appears (on paper) that they are major contributors to the fight against fraud. Experienced agents and investigators know who the coattailers are.

Many U.S. attorneys' offices across the country have healthcare fraud task forces or working groups that hold periodic meetings and work together or share information. I've personally attended some of those meetings, which included both civil and criminal federal prosecutors, federal agents, state investigators, and investigators from private insurance companies.

A number of federal agencies have their own investigative agents that investigate fraud, waste, and abuse affecting their agencies. In most instances, they are the experts or most knowledgeable about the insurance policies and procedures of their own agencies. Many of these federal agencies are from the Office of Inspector General (OIG). These OIGs have easier access to their own agencies' insurance claims, records of payment, listings of approved providers, and so forth. The same is true of each private insurance company.

Federal Offices of Inspector General

There are over 70 federal OIGs that investigate fraud, waste, and abuse. Listed here are only three that are known to investigate healthcare fraud on a large scale. The partial descriptions in italics were reprinted from their website postings in June 2015:

1. **Health and Human Services (HHS)**

> *Since its 1976 establishment, OIG has been at the forefront of the Nation's efforts to fight waste, fraud and abuse in Medicare, Medicaid and more than 100 other HHS programs.*
>
> *HHS OIG is the largest inspector general's office in the Federal Government, with approximately 1,600*

dedicated to combating fraud, waste and abuse and to improving the efficiency of HHS programs. A majority of OIG's resources goes toward the oversight of Medicare and Medicaid—programs that represent a significant part of the Federal budget and that affect this country's most vulnerable citizens. OIG's oversight extends to programs under other HHS institutions, including the Centers for Disease Control and Prevention, National Institutes of Health, and the Food and Drug Administration.

For more information, visit: http://oig.hhs.gov/about-oig/about-us/.

2. Department of Defense (DoD)

Author's Note: *The investigative arm of the DoD's OIG is called the Defense Criminal Investigative Service (DCIS). DCIS investigates healthcare fraud involving TRICARE, which is a government healthcare program that covers active duty military personnel, their dependants, and military retirees. Like all federal investigative agencies, DCIS's investigative priorities change as deemed appropriate by senior management.*

Mission—Protecting the Warfighter
Conduct highly relevant, objective, professional investigations of matters critical to DoD property, programs, and operations that provide for our national security with emphasis on life, safety, and readiness.

Investigative Priorities
Pursuant to the statutory obligations of the DoD Inspector General to "initiate, conduct, and supervise such ...investigations in the Department of Defense (including the military departments) as the Inspector General considers appropriate" (IG Act §8(c)(2)) and to "give particular regard to the activities of the internal ... investigative units of the military departments with a view toward avoiding duplication and insuring effective coordination and cooperation" (IG Act §8(c)(9)), the DCIS devotes investigative resources to:

- *Procurement Fraud and Public Corruption*
- *Product Substitution*
- *Health Care Fraud*
- *Illegal Technology Transfer*
- *Computer Crimes*

For more information, visit: http://www.dodig.mil/INV_DCIS/index.cfm.

3. Department of Veteran Affairs (VA)

> *The Office of Investigations (OI) investigates crimes committed against programs and operations of VA by employees and non-employees, as well as allegations of serious violations of policies and procedures by high-ranking members of the Department. OI is composed of four divisions: Criminal Investigations, Administrative Investigations, Analysis and Oversight, and Investigative Data Systems and Analysis. Criminal investigations focus on fraud against VA committed by beneficiaries, their survivors, fiduciaries, contractors, and VA employees; fraud related to pharmaceutical firms' illegal defective pricing or off-label marketing activities; acts of embezzlement, extortion, and bribery committed by VA employees; theft and diversion of legal drugs by VA staff and others; sale of contraband drugs and pharmaceuticals by and to VA staff and patients; theft of VA resources and data; identity theft; stolen valor; assaults involving VA employees and patients, including homicide, manslaughter, and rape; threats against VA employees, patients, facilities, and computer systems; mortgage fraud; workers' compensation fraud; and Service Disabled Veteran Owned Small Business (SDVOSB) fraud. Administrative investigations focus on violations of policies and procedures concerning high-ranking senior officials, such as misuse of Government resources and official time, preferential treatment, abuse of authority, nepotism, and travel irregularities. Through prosecution, administrative action, and monetary recoveries, these investigations promote integrity, patient safety, efficiency, and accountability.*

For more information, visit: http://www.va.gov/oig/about/investigations.asp.

Author's Note: *It must be emphasized that the three OIGs listed earlier are not the only federal OIGs that investigate healthcare fraud. All of the OIGs do an outstanding job of investigating fraud, waste, and abuse involving their agencies and often work jointly with many or all of the investigative agencies listed in this chapter.*

Other federal investigative agencies

There are also some federal investigative agencies that don't suffer financial losses because of healthcare fraud but often investigate or provide assistance during such investigations. A few are listed here. The descriptions in italics were reprinted from their websites in June 2015.

- **Food and Drug Administration (FDA)**

> *FDA is responsible for protecting the public health by assuring the safety, efficacy and security of human and veterinary drugs, biological products, medical devices, our nation's food supply, cosmetics, and products that emit radiation.*
>
> *FDA is also responsible for advancing the public health by helping to speed innovations that make medicines more effective, safer, and more affordable and by helping the public get the accurate, science-based information they need to use medicines and foods to maintain and improve their health. FDA also has responsibility for regulating the manufacturing, marketing and distribution of tobacco products to protect the public health and to reduce tobacco use by minors.*
>
> *Finally, FDA plays a significant role in the Nation's counterterrorism capability. FDA fulfills this responsibility by ensuring the security of the food supply and by fostering development of medical products to respond to deliberate and naturally emerging public health threats.*

For additional information, visit: http://www.fda.gov/AboutFDA/WhatWeDo/.

- **Drug Enforcement Administration (DEA)**

> *The mission of the Drug Enforcement Administration (DEA) is to enforce the controlled substances laws and regulations of the United States and bring to the criminal and civil justice system of the United States, or any other competent jurisdiction, those organizations and principal members of organizations, involved in the growing, manufacture, or distribution of controlled substances appearing in or destined for illicit traffic in the United States; and to recommend and support non-enforcement programs aimed at reducing the availability of illicit controlled substances on the domestic and international markets.*
>
> *In carrying out its mission as the agency responsible for enforcing the controlled substances laws and regulations of the United States, the DEA's primary responsibilities include:*

- *Investigation and preparation for the prosecution of major violators of controlled substance laws operating at interstate and international levels.*
- *Investigation and preparation for prosecution of criminals and drug gangs who perpetrate violence in our communities and terrorize citizens through fear and intimidation.*
- *Management of a national drug intelligence program in cooperation with federal, state, local, and foreign officials to collect, analyze, and disseminate strategic and operational drug intelligence information.*
- *Seizure and forfeiture of assets derived from, traceable to, or intended to be used for illicit drug trafficking.*
- *Enforcement of the provisions of the Controlled Substances Act as they pertain to the manufacture, distribution, and dispensing of legally produced controlled substances.*
- *Coordination and cooperation with federal, state and local law enforcement officials on mutual drug enforcement efforts and enhancement of such efforts through exploitation of potential interstate and international investigations beyond local or limited federal jurisdictions and resources.*
- *Coordination and cooperation with federal, state, and local agencies, and with foreign governments, in programs designed to reduce the availability of illicit abuse-type drugs on the United States market through nonenforcement methods such as crop eradication, crop substitution, and training of foreign officials.*
- *Responsibility, under the policy guidance of the Secretary of State and U.S. Ambassadors, for all programs associated with drug law enforcement counterparts in foreign countries.*
- *Liaison with the United Nations, Interpol, and other organizations on matters relating to international drug control programs.*

For additional information, visit: http://www.dea.gov/about/mission.shtml.

- **U.S. Postal Inspection Service (USPIS)**

Author's Note: *USPIS often assists in fraud investigations including healthcare fraud cases. Its nexus to those cases is that most fraudulent insurance claim forms (and payments) are sent electronically or via U.S. Postal Service.*

> *U.S. Postal Inspectors are federal law enforcement officers who carry firearms, make arrests, execute federal search warrants, and serve subpoenas. Inspectors work with U.S. Attorneys, other law enforcement, and local prosecutors to investigate cases and prepare them for court. Inspectors throughout the country enforce roughly 200 federal laws related to crimes that adversely affect or entail fraudulent use of the U.S. Postal Service the postal system, postal employees, and customers.*

For additional information, visit: https://postalinspectors.uspis.gov/aboutus/mission.aspx.

- **Federal Bureau of Investigation (FBI)**

Author's Note: *The FBI also conducts numerous healthcare fraud investigations even though its own agency is not ordinarily a victim of such fraud and investigating for waste, abuse is not part of its mission. Because they are our country's largest criminal investigative agency, the FBI has incredible resources, and their agents conduct their own investigations and assist others in healthcare fraud investigations. The FBI is the go-to agency if the case has international involvement. The information listed here was reprinted from the FBI's website in June 2015:*

> *Health care fraud costs the country tens of billions of dollars a year. It's a rising threat, with national health care expenditures estimated to exceed $3 trillion in 2014 and spending continuing to outpace inflation. Recent cases also show that medical professionals continue, and may be more willing, to risk patient harm in furtherance of their schemes. The FBI is the primary agency for exposing and investigating health care fraud, with jurisdiction over both federal and private insurance programs. We seek to identify and pursue investigations against the most egregious offenders involved in health care fraud through our investigative partnerships with federal, state, and local agencies, as well as our relationships with private insurance national groups, associations, and investigative units. Our field offices proactively target fraud through coordinated initiatives, task forces and strike teams, and undercover operations.*

For additional information, visit: http://www.fbi.gov/about-us/investigate/white_collar/health-care-fraud.

State investigative agencies

States also have their own investigative agencies or bureaus of investigation that investigate healthcare fraud. Some states (perhaps all) have investigative teams, which they may call a "Medicaid Task Force."

Private insurance investigators

Private insurance companies also have their own investigative teams, which are often referred to as Special Investigative Units (SIUs) and they often work closely with federal and state investigators.

National Insurance Crime Bureau

The National Insurance Crime Bureau also provides member organizations with assistance in healthcare fraud investigative efforts. For additional information, visit: www.nicb.org.

Project On Government Oversight

I first learned about the Project On Government Oversight (POGO) in 2006, while serving as a federal agent after I initiated a corrupt procurement investigation involving some of the highest ranking U.S. military officers. The case involved the awarding of a $50 million government contract. While watching the national news, I saw a POGO investigator telling a reporter all about my new case. Apparently, POGO received information about the matter and dug into it long before I received any information about the wrongdoing. I will add that everything that the POGO investigator related on the news was right on the money. My point is the general public needs to become more aware of POGO. The information provided here in italics was reprinted from POGO's website in June 2015:

> ***ABOUT POGO:***
> *Founded in 1981, POGO originally worked to expose outrageously overpriced military spending on items such as a $7,600 coffee maker and a $436 hammer. In 1990, after many successes reforming military spending, including a Pentagon spending freeze at the height of the Cold War, POGO decided to expand its mandate and investigate waste, fraud, and abuse throughout the federal government.*
>
> *Throughout its history, POGO's work has been applauded by Members of Congress from both sides of the*

aisle, federal workers and whistleblowers, other nonprofits, and the media.

POGO's Mission:
Founded in 1981, the Project On Government Oversight (POGO) is a nonpartisan independent watchdog that champions good government reforms. POGO's investigations into corruption, misconduct, and conflicts of interest achieve a more effective, accountable, open, and ethical federal government.

How POGO Works:

- *IDENTIFIES systemic corruption, undue influence, or other misconduct impacting the federal government*
- *Launches independent INVESTIGATIONS into cases that meet POGO guidelines*
- *Conducts research and works with whistleblowers and other insiders to INVESTIGATE TIPS and DOCUMENT FINDINGS*
- *Recommends COMMON-SENSE SOLUTIONS for positive change*
- *EDUCATES MEDIA AND THE PUBLIC of findings and EMPOWERS THE PUBLIC TO ACT*
- *Works with government officials to IMPLEMENT SYSTEMIC POLICY IMPROVEMENTS*
- *Strives for a more EFFECTIVE, ACCOUNTABLE, OPEN, AND ETHICAL federal government*

How POGO Chooses Its Projects:
The following are the guidelines by which POGO determines which projects we pursue. They do not present rigid criteria but provide us with a consistent way to evaluate our priorities.

- *Capacity to make a unique contribution*
- *Opening for positive systemic change in the federal government*
- *Ability to broaden public awareness*
- *Urgency for action*
- *Availability of inside sources and documents*

POGO'S Methodology:
While some groups are staffed with scientists or experts who focus on a single issue, POGO is an investigative organization with an expertise for working with sources

> *inside the government and whistleblowers to document evidence of corruption, waste, fraud, or abuse. Many of our nation's most dedicated citizens work in and around the federal government. When they come across information revealing serious misconduct, they rightfully believe that they would risk losing their job if they came forward and "blew the whistle" on the wrongdoing they see. According to government surveys, one out of every 14 federal employees reported being retaliated against in a two-year period for making disclosures concerning health and safety dangers; unlawful behavior; and fraud, waste, and abuse.*
>
> *POGO's investigators and journalists take leads and information from insiders and verify the information through investigations using the Freedom of Information Act, interviews, and other fact-finding strategies. We then disseminate our findings to the media, Congress, and public interest groups through alerts, statements, studies, and journalistic reports.*

For additional information, visit: www.pogo.org.

Others

There are others who assist in the investigation of healthcare fraud. For example, some companies that sell pharmaceuticals have their own investigators or investigative annalysts as well as risk management experts. Federal and state prosecutor offices (criminal and civil) often employ (or contract out) the services of healthcare fraud investigators, examiners, analysts, auditors, and so forth. Knowledgeable private investigators and consultants also often provide assistance to attorneys, whistleblowers, and others in healthcare fraud matters and provide training.

Healthcare fraud investigation certifications and credentials

There are several organizations that provide training and/or professional certifications or designations that are highly respected in the industry of investigating healthcare fraud.

- *Federal and state criminal investigators* are graduates of their own investigative academies. State investigators are Peace Officers Standards and Training (POST) certified meaning that they meet their state's Commission on Peace Officers Standards and Training. The law enforcement officers who investigate healthcare fraud complete additional training to keep abreast of the latest schemes, applicable laws, and other related information.

- The *Association of Certified Fraud Examiners* (*ACFE*) provides not only antifraud training but also the opportunity for individuals to become Certified Fraud Examiners (CFE). The CFE designation is an internationally known and respected designation for fraud fighters—including many healthcare fraud fighters. Some federal, state, and local law enforcement agencies as well as private sector organizations seek applicants who have earned or are pursuing the CFE credential and often encourage current fraud fighters within their organizations to pursue the credential. For additional information, visit: www.acfe.com.
- The *National Health Care Anti-Fraud Association* (*NHCAA*) provides training focused on fighting healthcare fraud. It also provides individuals the opportunity to become certified as Accredited Health Care Fraud Investigators (AHFI). Their website refers to this credential as "The gold standard designation in health care fraud investigation." For additional information, visit: www.nhcaa.org.

Author's Note: *It must be emphasized that not all of the professionals that fight healthcare fraud have "investigator" or "special agent" in their job title and many of them hold the designation of CFE or AHFI. For example, nurses and other healthcare professionals often provide their valued expertise in healthcare fraud investigations and examinations. Analysts, examiners, attorneys, accountants, computer and software experts, consultants, and others are instrumental in the team effort of fighting healthcare fraud.*

WAR STORY 4.2

While reviewing several different databases containing information on healthcare providers' claims and payments, I strove valiantly to query and search for patterns and trends to identify possible fraud. Based on my own previous experiences, I knew it would take me several hours to identify all the information I wanted. An analyst, who never served a single day in law enforcement and never conducted an interview or interrogation in their life, offered assistance and obtained all of the information I wanted and more in less than 30 minutes. Some analysts can search, sort, and filter as fast as some grocery store clerks scan items at the cash register. The best way to combat healthcare fraud is to work as a team and make use of all resources—Don't forget to say please and thank you!

Complainants

Where do complaints that result in criminal and civil fraud investigations originate? In 2014, the Association of Certified Fraud Examiners (ACFE) completed an Annual Global Fraud Study regarding occupational fraud that included many different occupational fraud schemes. It was not a study exclusive to healthcare fraud, but it provides an idea where complaints about fraud originate. Two of the findings are listed here.

(The following was reprinted from the ACFE's 2014 Global Fraud Study—Report to the Nations on Occupational Fraud and Abuse.)

1. Tips are consistently and by far the most common detection method. Over 40% of all cases were detected by a tip—more than twice the rate of any other detection method. Employees accounted for nearly half of all tips that led to the discovery of fraud.
2. Organizations with hotlines were much more likely to catch fraud by a tip, which our data show is the most effective way to detect fraud. These organizations also experienced frauds that were 41 percent less costly, and they detected frauds 50 percent more quickly.

Other lesser methods of detection identified in ACFE's study included (in order):

- Internal audit
- Management review
- Account reconciliation
- By accident
- Surveillance or monitoring
- Document examination
- External audit
- Notified by law enforcement
- Information Technology (IT) controls
- Confession
- Others

In the 20 years I served as a federal agent, the four most common sources for healthcare fraud complaints that resulted in my opening new criminal or civil investigations were hotline complaints (sometimes from anonymous callers), whistleblower complaints, internal audits (including referrals from program integrity offices), and spin-offs of other open or recently closed inner agency investigations (including spin-offs of investigative projects that were opened for the purpose of identifying fraud).

Referrals from other investigative agencies were actually uncommon, which is remarkable considering the large number of investigative entities and organizations that investigate healthcare fraud. I think most would agree that investigative organizations do not always work together as often as they could.

People make formal complaints about healthcare fraud for a variety of reasons including but not limited to just wanting to do the right thing, to eliminate competition, to avoid personal loss or harm, to profit from the investigation, for revenge, other reasons, or all or some of the aforementioned reasons. One of those probably caught your eye: "to profit from the investigation."

Whistleblowers can often make money (*share in a percentage of the dollar recovery*) if an investigation is initiated and successfully concluded (with dollar recoveries) based on information the whistleblower provides. This is sometimes referred to as a *writ of qui tam* or simply as a *qui tam* action. *Qui tam* stems from a Latin phrase which means, "[he] who sues in this matter for the king as well as for himself." There are many prerequisites that must be met before a whistleblower can financially benefit in the dollar recoveries.

Since retiring from federal service and opening my own private investigation and consulting company, I have come into contact with many experienced attorneys and law firms that actually specialize in handling whistleblower (*qui tam*) cases. Some of those attorneys previously served as federal civil prosecutors that handled healthcare fraud cases—so they know the ropes.

In my current capacity, I have had the pleasure of assisting in and putting together potential whistleblower actions, which include conducting well-planned and thorough interviews of the complainants and legally obtaining factual information about the suspect providers and their healthcare organizations. In addition to utilizing many subscription databases, I have found that the amount of public information available over the Internet about providers and the organizations is actually staggering. The purpose of the thorough preliminary investigative or consulting work is to compile all of the information so that the whistleblower attorney(s) can file their case in court with as much supportive documentation and information as possible with hopes that the government will intervene and initiate an investigation. Besides accomplishing justice, a lot of people that put the original complaint together can also make money.

WAR STORY 4.3

While working as a private investigator and consultant, some clients have asked me to work on a contingency basis where I'd get paid a handsome percentage of any (possible) future recovery. I've always refused, because in my opinion, that would be a conflict of interest. My job is to identify facts, and I request payment for the work I do in advance and get paid the same hourly or daily fee regardless of the outcome. In essence, this is the same approach I used when serving as a federal agent. The investigator should never have a stake in the results of the investigation. However, it should be noted that in the real world, law enforcement agents and investigators often receive awards, bonuses, promotions, and high ratings on their evaluations when the investigations they conduct result in indictments, convictions, judgments, and dollar recoveries. In illegal drug and some other cases, law enforcement agencies and organizations often benefit financially from asset forfeitures in which just about anything used in the commission of the crime or that is purchased with the illegally obtained proceeds can be recovered by the government. Sometimes, the items recovered are sold at auctions. Asset forfeiture is a very lucrative source of income for many law enforcement agencies and organizations. The government often hires financial analysts on a contract basis for the purpose of identifying a suspect's assets, which are often hidden or difficult to trace.

Author's Note: *My book,* Investigator and Fraud Fighter Guidebook: Operation War Stories,* *details the importance of conducting as many as 10 related types of investigations simultaneously on each case worked. A diagram outlining "The Piper Method"* is provided at the beginning of this book. During my 30-year law enforcement career, I found great success using the information obtained from individual investigations to open separate new investigations to pursue additional suspects for committing the same types of violations as originally investigated. It's my strong belief that spin-off cases, proactive investigative projects, and referrals from other investigative agencies and organizations should be the top sources to generate new healthcare provider fraud cases.*

Undercover operations

In healthcare and other fraud cases, law enforcement sometimes conducts undercover operations that result in legally obtaining incriminating audio and/or video recordings, which help strengthen cases. However, sometimes, undercover activity can fail to produce the results expected.

* Piper, Charles E., *Investigator and Fraud Fighter Guidebook: Operation War Stories*, John Wiley & Sons, Hoboken, NJ, 2014. (Copyright 2014, Wiley-VCH Verlag GmbH & Co. KGaA. Reproduced with permission.)

WAR STORY 4.4

As a junior federal agent, I was tasked by a more senior agent to work undercover. I was told to pose as a patient. The senior agent previously received a tip that a particular medical doctor knowingly and intentionally wrote a false diagnosis on a patient who feigned a back injury to collect workers' compensation. My assignment was to see if the doctor would do the same for me after I told him there was nothing wrong with me and that I just needed the time off from work so that I could secretly work at another job and make more money. I was wearing a body recorder, which in retrospect probably wasn't the best choice but that's what I was instructed to wear.

I told the doctor that there was nothing wrong with me but I wanted him to sign a document saying that I had a back injury so that I could get time off my primary job, collect pay, and then get a second job on the side so that I could pay child support. Surprisingly, even after I told the doctor that there was nothing wrong with me, he asked me to get undressed. Frankly, I didn't feel like getting undressed. Besides, I was also wearing a body recorder. I told the doctor that there was no reason for me to get undressed because there was nothing wrong with me. Then the doctor suggested that I leave his office and that there would be no charge for the visit.

My suspicion is that if I had gotten undressed, the doctor probably would have written the false documents. But it wasn't like I volunteered for that particular assignment, and the oath I took as a law enforcement officer didn't say anything about getting naked for doctors.

Author's Note: *From firsthand experience gained while serving as a federal agent, I learned that a particular federal investigative agency that conducts mostly criminal investigations relies heavily on conducting undercover activity with hidden recorders to catch white collar criminals—as compared to performing the tedious (but necessary) task of reviewing documents. Granted, undercover activity is much more fun and appealing and makes for more sensational press releases, but history has shown that when working white collar cases, document review and analysis often results in not only criminal prosecutions but also in high-dollar civil recoveries. Performing undercover activity and conducting the necessary document review often allow for the best results.*

Although the benefits of using computer analytics and data mining will be mentioned in more detail later in this book, it's worth mentioning here that those tools (and the fraud fighters that utilize them) are invaluable in identifying fraud indicators (red flags) and actual fraud.

Laws and statutes

Let me preface the following by emphasizing that I am not an attorney and I am not offering legal guidance or advice on what charges or statutes to use during your investigations. (*This is a CYA note.*) Factually, there are many criminal and civil statutes that are violated in healthcare fraud cases. Ones to consider are federal, state, or local. Always remember that investigations into these matters can often be pursued criminally and civilly—often simultaneously (called parallel proceedings). Only considering the use of criminal charges on your healthcare provider cases would (in my opinion) be shortsighted. An exception might be when you know for certain that the suspect is dead broke (indigent). It would behoove investigators to familiarize themselves with all criminal and civil statutes that might be applicable when conducting healthcare fraud investigations.

While attending the federal law enforcement academy, my classmates and I received training on various topics including law, criminal procedure, the rules of evidence, and so forth. We were taught to read the "elements of proof" of federal criminal and civil statutes to ensure we had (or pursued and found) evidence supporting all of those elements in order to prove the wrongdoing that might be charged. If such evidence did not exist, then the statute(s) should not be used.

For example, for the criminal charge of making a "false claim" under Title 18, United States Code (USC) 287, the government must establish that the defendant

- *Made or presented a false, fictitious, or fraudulent claim to a department of the United States*
- *Knew such claim was false, fictitious, or fraudulent*
- *Did so with the specific intent to violate the law or with a consciousness that what he was doing was wrong*

If charged with a false claim, the defendant could be fined (not more than $5000), or imprisoned for no more than 5 years, or both.

Author's Note: *If charged with the criminal offense of "Conspiracy to Defraud the Government with respect to Claims" (Title 18 USC 286) (meaning two or more people acting together) they could be fined or imprisoned for not more than 10 years or both.*

A civil offense to also consider would be the Civil False Claims Act (31 U.S.C. §§ 3729–3733). If this statute is followed, it must be shown that "the defendant submitted, or caused the submission of, the false claim (or made a false statement or record) with knowledge of the falsity."

False information is defined as being "(1) actual knowledge, (2) deliberate ignorance of the truth or falsity of the information, or (3) reckless disregard of the truth or falsity of the information."

The False Claims Act says, "a claim is a demand for money or property made directly to the Federal Government or to a contractor, grantee, or other recipient if the money is to spent on the government's behalf and if the Federal Government provides any of the money demanded or if the Federal Government will reimburse the contractor or grantee."

Regarding damages and penalties under the False Claims Act, if one is found liable, they must pay a civil penalty of between $5,000 and $10,000 for each false claim (those amounts are sometimes adjusted) and up to three times the amount of the government's damages.

Obviously, the civil statute would be much easier to prove, and with the potential awarding of damages of up three times the dollar amount of each false claim, the dollar recovery could be huge! In short, focusing solely on criminal violations is often shortsighted. *Why not pursue both?*

My limited research has found that many (if not all) states have their own criminal and civil false claims statutes (or equivalent). For example, the state of Tennessee has the following:

- 71-5-181: TN Medicaid False Claims Act (includes TENNCARE)
- 4-18-101: TN False Claims Act

The assigned prosecutors will be the ones to make the final decision as to which charges to consider. But if you read the statutes and their elements of proof, you can investigate and present your case in a more professional and knowledgeable manner.

WAR STORY 4.5

During my federal law enforcement career, I found that some criminal prosecutors try to dictate the investigative course of action even if it means jeopardizing the potential civil case. For example, in a federal case, once grand jury subpoenas are used to obtain testimony or records, the testimony obtained (and often the records obtained) cannot be used in the civil proceedings. Very often, the investigators could have just as easily used administrative subpoenas to obtain records or conducted interviews without subpoenas. Then, the documents and verbal statements could be used in both the criminal and civil cases. But some criminal prosecutors will sometimes still insist that grand jury subpoenas be used. The investigative agencies that focus primarily on criminal cases (and not civil cases) often happily agree with those criminal prosecutors about using grand jury subpoenas.

Author's Note: *Because of this potential issue, investigators might want to learn the criminal prosecutor's stance early during the investigation regarding the use of your investigative tools that better assist in obtaining the best overall outcome for the investigation criminally and civilly.*

Federal statutes to consider

Listed here is a list of federal criminal and civil statutes that might be considered when investigating or prosecuting healthcare fraud cases. It is not inclusive of all possible statutes. Individual states may have similar or other statutes to consider. Please consult and review the actual statutes and sources.

The *Health Insurance Portability and Accountability Act* (*HIPAA*) of 1996 established several criminal statutes relating specifically to healthcare fraud. HIPAA also established security and privacy of healthcare data requirements.

Author's Note: *If you are investigating healthcare fraud, make sure you become familiar with HIPPA—especially regarding your responsibilities of protecting the privacy of healthcare patient data.*

HIPPA provides that a judge can order a person convicted of a federal healthcare offense to forfeit any property that can be traced from the proceeds received from the offense (See 18 USC 1345).

Federal criminal statutes

18 USA 1347:	Healthcare Fraud
18 USC 1345:	Freeze Assets of HC Fraud Prior to Conviction.
18 USC 669:	Steal/Theft or Embezzle Healthcare Benefit Program
18 USC 1035:	False Statements Relating to Healthcare Matters
18 USC 1518:	Obstruction of Criminal Investigation of Healthcare Matters
18 USC 1956:	Healthcare Money Laundering
42 USC 1320 a-7b (b):	Federal Healthcare Anti-Kickback Act (applies to anyone)
18 USC 1001:	False Statement (Oral, Written)
18 USC 1002:	False Papers
18 USC 371:	Conspiracy

18 USC 286:	Conspiracy Claims
18 USC 287:	False Claim (does not have to be paid)
18 USC 1030:	Computer Fraud
18 USC 1956:	Money Laundering
18 USC 1028:	Identity Theft—False ID
18 USC 1341:	1343 (Mail and Wire Fraud)
18 USC 1342:	Fictitious name or address
18 USC 1345:	Freeze Assets of HC Fraud Prior to Conviction
18 USC 1510:	Obstruction of Criminal Investigation
18 USC 1512:	Tampering with Witness, Victim, or Informant
18 USC 1516:	Obstruction of a Federal Audit
15 USC 16p3n:	(Paperless money transfers between accounts)
15 USC 1644:	False Credit Card
18 USC 2326:	Senior Citizen Marketing Scams
21 USC 841:	Drug Charges
21 USC 846:	Conspiracy to Distribute Controlled Substances
18 USC 1344:	Bank Fraud
18 USC 4:	Misprision of a Felony
18 USC 1961–1968:	Racketeer Influenced and Corrupt Organizations (RICO) Statute
18 USC 1345:	Freeze Assets of HC Fraud Prior to Conviction.

Author's Note: *The False Claims Act and RICO provide for both criminal penalties and civil remedies.*

Federal civil statutes

- *31 USC 3729-3733 Civil False Claims Act*: (False Claims) This statute also allows private parties to prosecute civil action against perpetrators(s) on behalf of the government.
- *31 USC 3801-3812: Program Fraud Civil Remedies*: Includes False Claims and the collection of civil penalties and assessments.
- *42 USC 1320a-7a Civil Monetary Penalties Law*: Administrative action can be invoked against providers who defraud any federally funded program by filing false claims or other improper billing practices—Can be fined up to $10 K for each medical service that was fraudulently represented and they can be excluded from participating in government programs.

Additional federal statutes

42 USC 1395 N The Stark Law (*Stark Act*): (applies to physician referrals). A physician cannot refer (clinical lab or designated health services) to anyone who the physician or immediate family member has a financial relationship ($15 K–$100 K). Also prohibits the referral receiver from submitting a claim to Medicare or Medicaid.

The Park Doctrine: Individuals and executives of corporations can be held liable for first-time misdemeanor and possible subsequent felony under the Park Doctrine. Too often, corporations are charged criminally time after time but nothing happens to the responsible executives. Utilizing the Park Doctrine can change all that.

The FDA's Compliance, Enforcement, and Criminal Investigations Manual (Section 6.5 on Prosecution) provides information about the Park Doctrine. The following was reprinted from its website in June 2015:

> *The Park Doctrine, as established by Supreme Court case law, provides that a responsible corporate official can be held liable for a first time misdemeanor (and possible subsequent felony) under the Federal Food, Drug, and Cosmetic Act ("the Act") without proof that the corporate official acted with intent or even negligence, and even if such corporate official did not have any actual knowledge of, or participation in, the specific offense. A Park Doctrine prosecution, for the purposes of this section, refers to a recommended prosecution of a responsible corporate official for a misdemeanor violation of the Act.*
>
> *Misdemeanor prosecution under the Act can be a valuable enforcement tool. Such prosecutions are referred to the Department of Justice. Once a person has been convicted of a misdemeanor under the Act, any subsequent violation of the Act is a felony, even without proof that the defendant acted with the intent to defraud or mislead. Misdemeanor prosecutions, particularly those against responsible corporate officials, can have a strong deterrent effect on the defendants and other regulated entities. In some cases, a misdemeanor conviction of an individual may serve as the basis for debarment by FDA.*
>
> *When considering whether to recommend a misdemeanor prosecution against a corporate official, consider the individual's position in the company and relationship to the violation, and whether the official had the authority to correct or prevent the violation. Knowledge of and actual participation in the violation are not a prerequisite to a misdemeanor prosecution but are factors that may be relevant when deciding whether to recommend charging a misdemeanor violation.*

Other factors to consider include but are not limited to:

1. *Whether the violation involves actual or potential harm to the public;*
2. *Whether the violation is obvious;*
3. *Whether the violation reflects a pattern of illegal behavior or failure to heed prior warnings;*
4. *Whether the violation is widespread;*
5. *Whether the violation is serious;*
6. *The quality of the legal and factual support for the proposed prosecution; and*
7. *Whether the proposed prosecution is a prudent use of agency resources.*

As the Supreme Court has recognized, it would be futile to attempt to define or indicate by way of illustration either the categories of persons that may bear a responsible relationship to a violation or the types of conduct that may be viewed as causing or contributing to a violation of the Act. In addition, these factors are intended solely for the guidance of FDA personnel, do not create or confer any rights or benefits for or on any person, and do not operate to bind FDA. Further, the absence of some factors does not mean that a referral is inappropriate where other factors are evident.

When a district office is considering initiating a referral for a Park Doctrine prosecution, the district is required to consult with the appropriate center to ensure that the referral will align with agency priorities and that the center will support the referral and provide expert witnesses or other litigation support when necessary. Centers and district offices are also encouraged to consult with OCC and OCI HQ Special Agent in Charge (SAIC) or the Assistant Special Agent in Charge (ASAIC) Investigative Operations Division (IOD) early in the process for guidance and recommendations regarding optimal venue…

For additional information, visit: http://www.fda.gov/ICECI/ComplianceManuals/RegulatoryProceduresManual/ucm176738.htm.

The *Affordable Care Act* has received more than its share of praise and criticism. But as far as fighting fraud goes, some improvements have been made. Listed here are just a few:

- There has been increased funding to fight healthcare fraud.
- There is more sharing of information to fight healthcare fraud (integrated data repository between Medicaid, VA, DoD, and Medicare; access to claims and payment databases).
- Enhancement of tools to detect healthcare fraud.
- Increases to provider and others' screening and other enrollment requirements.
- Providers and suppliers are required to detail how they will prevent fraud (and surety bonds are required).
- With credible allegations, payments may be suspended (rather than "pay and chase").
- Overpayment recovery efforts have been expanded.
- Federal sentencing guidelines have been increased.
- Penalties for healthcare fraud violations have been increased—including termination from programs.

More on healthcare fraud fighters

People have often said to me, "You look like a cop." Sometimes, I can even spot other law enforcement and investigative personnel just by the way they carry themselves. Healthcare fraud fighters perform their duties in many different capacities including as investigators, auditors, annalists, consultants, and so forth. But there are some helpful ways to determine if you or someone else might be a healthcare fraud fighter. As in the last two chapters, I'll provide this information in comedian Jeff Foxworthy fashion by giving this topic a subheading of

You might be a healthcare fraud fighter if

- Every time you watch *The Cosby Show* on television, you wonder if Dr. Huxtable is billing for patient care while he's sitting around in his living room during the daytime
- You closely review your own Explanation of Benefits forms hoping your doctor billed for something the doctor did not do
- Your Christmas wish lists includes a copy of the ACFE's Fraud Manual and annual dues payment to the NHCAA
- You wonder why the senior citizen's retirement community is located next door to a funeral home
- You think "open season" means it's time to go hunting for corrupt physicians
- You frequently call the Medicare fraud hotline and ask, "What's new?"
- You always wonder if your dentist really put in the number fillings listed on the claim form

- You think the tooth fairy and your kid's orthodontist are involved in a conspiracy
- Every time you enter a hospital building, you check your wallet
- Every time you leave a hospital building, you check your wallet
- You think "double date" means billing two separate days for the same medical treatment
- Every time you see an adult riding on their own scooter, you wonder how much Medicare paid for it
- You thought the movie *Life of Pi* was going to be about a private investigator
- You wonder why healthcare still isn't affordable since they passed the Affordable Care Act
- You'd much rather analyze healthcare claim forms than read the sports page
- You often wonder if Doctor Spock who wrote the book on baby and child care ever had pointed ears
- You seriously think that dentists invented *trick-or-treating*
- You always count the number of pills the pharmacist gives you before you leave the drug store
- You lose sleep wondering if Doctor Scholl is an actual doctor
- When taking a physical, you refuse to look the other way when the doctor says, "Cough."
- You think the nurse who inflates the blood pressure cup around your arm intentionally tries to cut off your circulation
- The only doctor you trust is named Pepper and comes in a can

All kidding aside, with the combined efforts and contributions by many, teamwork and the use of tools, resources, and funding, fraud fighters have and will continue to make great strides to combating healthcare fraud. Continued training, sharing of information and learning from others, allow for healthcare fraud investigations to be conducted more efficiently and maximize results.

The next chapter details healthcare codes, numbers, abbreviations, forms, and documents. (*Yes, this might be a good time to get a cup of coffee.*)

chapter five

Codes, numbers, forms, and documents

Codes and numbers

The healthcare industry has codes and numbers that describe anything and everything that is billed for—from bandages to brain surgery. In the United States, each provider and the medical facility where they work is required to obtain their own unique National Provider Identifier (NPI), which is a unique 10-digit identification number. The NPIs are issued by the Centers for Medicare and Medicaid Services (CMS). The provider's NPI is assigned to them permanently even if they change jobs or locations. Physicians, nurses, dentists, physical therapists, pharmacies, laboratories, medical equipment companies, and more must get their own unique NPI.

Author's Note: *When analyzing fraudulent insurance claim forms along with patient charts and doctor notes, I've noticed that the NPIs listed on claim forms are not always indicative of who actually provided the services. For example, "Provider A" may have provided the services, which were supervised by "Dr. B" and they both worked at "Clinic C," which is owned by "Dr. D." Some of the insurance claim forms might list the NPI for "Provider A," some might list "Dr. B," some might list "Clinic C," and some might list "Dr. D."*

If you are running a query or preparing to conduct an audit, subpoena request, search warrant, or other requests or demands for the purpose of identifying all claims or services provided by a specific provider(s), you may want to consider using broad parameters so that you are more likely to find or obtain everything you are looking for.

Types of codes

The following is a list of some of the categories of codes or numbers that you are likely to come across while investigating healthcare fraud. Note that some billing codes are subject to change.

- *HCPCS (pronounced: "Hicks Picks")*: Healthcare Common Procedural Coding System. Included are both Current Procedural Terminology (CPT) medical codes (as described in later text) and nonmedical codes (i.e., specific items and services provided when delivering canes, bandages, injections, prosthetics, Durable Medical Equipment [DME], etc.). The codes are used in both public and private insurance plans

- *CPT*: Current Procedural Terminology (Treatment and Diagnostic Services)
- *ICD-9*: International Classification of Diseases (Symptoms and Diagnoses)
- *NDC*: National Drug Code (11 digits, 3 segments)

The following are a few CPT codes and what they stand for.

CPT code examples: Psychotherapy

- *90791*: Psychiatric diagnostic evaluation
- *90792*: Psychiatric diagnostic evaluation with medical services, E/M

New Patient codes may also be used

- *90832*: Psychotherapy 30 (16–37) minutes
- *90834*: Psychotherapy 45 (38–52) minutes
- *90837*: Psychotherapy 60 (53+) minutes
- *90839*: Psychotherapy for crisis, first 60 minutes
- *+90840*: Add-on for each additional 30 minutes of crisis therapy
- *+90863*: Pharmacologic management, including prescription and review of meds; used *only* as an add-on to Primary Psychotherapy codes (90832, 90834, 90837)

You probably observed in the earlier examples that the amount of time spent with a patient dictates which CPT code to use for billing purposes. For example, different codes are required when increasing from 37 to 38 minutes or from 52 to 53 minutes. The more minutes utilized, the more the provider can bill for. (*Hmm…Seems like it would be pretty easy to spend an extra minute here and there to make a few more bucks, doesn't it?*)

Listed in the following are a few HCPCS codes and what they stand for.

HCPCS code examples: Wheelchairs

- *K0001*: Standard wheelchair
- *K0002*: Standard hemi (low seat) wheelchair
- *K0003*: Lightweight wheelchair
- *K0004*: High-strength, lightweight wheelchair
- *K0005*: Ultralightweight wheelchairs
- *K0006*: Heavy-duty wheelchair
- *K0007*: Extra-heavy-duty wheelchair
- *K0009*: Other manual wheelchair/base
- *K0010*: Standard-weight frame motorized/power wheelchair

- *K0011*: Standard-weight frame motorized/power wheelchair with programmable control parameters for speed adjustment, tremor dampening, acceleration control, and braking
- *K0012*: Lightweight portable motorized/power wheelchair
- *K0014*: Other motorized/power wheelchair base
- *E0983*: Manual wheelchair accessory, power add-on to convert manual wheelchair to motorized wheelchair, joystick control
- *E0984*: Manual wheelchair accessory, power add-on to convert manual wheelchair to motorized wheelchair, tiller control
- *E2368*: Power wheelchair component, motor, replacement only
- *E2369*: Power wheelchair component, gearbox, replacement only
- *E2370*: Power wheelchair component, motor and gearbox combination, replacement only

Author's Note: *There are many additional wheelchair-related HCPCS codes that include items like footrests, arm pads, spoke protectors, IV hangers, replacement batteries, and so forth.*

You probably observed that changing one or two digits can make a difference in what is claimed and how much money is received. For example, HCPCS code K0001 is for a standard wheelchair and code K0010 is for a motorized or powered wheelchair. There is a lot more money involved with powered wheelchairs.

Abbreviations and acronyms

Although there are dozens of healthcare abbreviations or acronyms that could be included in this writing, listed here are four that you will definitely need to know:

- *CMS*: Centers for Medicare and Medicaid Services—CMS is a federal agency within the United States Department of Health and Human Services that "covers 100 million people through Medicare, Medicaid, the Children's Health Insurance Program, and the Health Insurance Marketplace." (Reprinted from cms.gov.)
- *HMO*: Health Maintenance Organization—"In most HMO Plans, you can only go to doctors, other health care providers, or hospitals on the plan's list except in an emergency. You may also need to get a referral from your primary care doctor." (Reprinted from Medicare.gov.)
- *PPO*: Preferred Provider Organization—"In a PPO Plan, you pay less if you use doctors, hospitals, and other health care providers that belong to the plan's network. You pay more if you use doctors, hospitals, and providers outside of the network." (Reprinted from Medicare.gov.)
- *CMS 1500*: Insurance Claim Form (Previously used HCFA 1500)—"The CMS-1500 form is the official standard Medicare and Medicaid health insurance claim form required by the Centers for

> Medicare & Medicaid Services (CMS) of the U.S. Department of Health & Human Services. It was developed by the independent National Uniform Claim Committee (NUCC) and used by all noninstitutional medical provider or supplier to bill Medicare carriers and durable medical equipment regional carriers (DMERCs) when a provider qualifies for a waiver from the Administrative Simplification Compliance Act (ASCA) requirement for electronic submission of claims. It is also used for billing of some Medicaid State Agencies (contact your Medicaid State Agency for more details).
>
> Claims must be submitted on original, not photocopied, print versions of the CMS-1500 forms as they are printed in special OCR-scannable red ink. Original, blank forms are available from GPO in several convenient laser-printed compatible quantities and formats, such as single sheet, 1-part, 2-part, and 2-part snapout versions." (Reprinted from the U.S. Government Bookstore, http://bookstore.gpo.gov/catalog/health-benefits/health-insurance-claim-forms.)

Investigating healthcare insurance fraud can sometimes feel a bit overwhelming. Based on my own years of experience, observations and interactions with most other investigators and special agents I worked with, you should feel comfortable knowing that you do not need to know "everything" about health insurance to successfully investigate healthcare fraud.

However, the more you know the better off you will be. Make sure you understand the victim insurance company and government program policies and procedures regarding the matter you are investigating. This means you may have to conduct your own research (some of which can often be obtained from the Internet) and ask questions of knowledgeable people in the industry. Government programs and insurance companies have their own program integrity units, risk management units (or similar names), which will be able to provide you with valuable assistance. Their company or government program may have lost money due to the fraud, so they will want to help you. In fact, it's often part of their job to help you if you work for or are protecting the agency/organization.

About Medicare

To provide a general idea about health insurance coverage and plans and what they include (and don't include), I selected Medicare as an example. In this writing, I've elected to provide information directly from the source. The following information in italics was reprinted in June 2015 directly from Medicare's website (medicare.gov). The information provided here is not all inclusive, and depending on when you read this book, the following information may have changed. (For the latest information, visit: medicare.gov.)

> *Medicare covers services (like lab tests, surgeries, and doctor visits) and supplies (like wheelchairs and walkers) considered medically necessary to treat a disease or condition.*
>
> *If you're in a Medicare Advantage Plan or other Medicare plan, you may have different rules, but your plan must give you at least the same coverage as Original Medicare. Some services may only be covered in certain settings or for patients with certain conditions.*
>
> ***In general, Part A covers:***
>
> - *Hospital care*
> - *Skilled nursing facility care*
> - *Nursing home care (as long as custodial care isn't the only care you need)*
> - *Hospice*
> - *Home health services*
>
> ***Part B covers 2 types of services:***
>
> - *Medically necessary services: Services or supplies that are needed to diagnose or treat your medical condition and that meet accepted standards of medical practice.*
> - *Preventive services: Health care to prevent illness (like the flu) or detect it at an early stage, when treatment is most likely to work best.*
>
> *You pay nothing for most preventive services if you get the services from a health care provider who accepts assignment.*
>
> ***Part B covers things like:***
>
> - *Clinical research*
> - *Ambulance services*
> - *Durable medical equipment (DME)*
> - *Mental health*
> - *Inpatient*
> - *Outpatient*
> - *Partial hospitalization*
> - *Getting a second opinion before surgery*
> - *Limited outpatient prescription drugs*

Part C includes both Part A (Hospital Insurance) and Part B (Medical Insurance)

Who provides coverage?
Private insurance companies approved by Medicare provide this coverage.

How do you choose your providers?
In most plans, you need to use plan doctors, hospitals, and other providers or you pay more or all of the costs.

Who pays the premiums?
You usually pay a monthly premium (in addition to your Part B premium).

Who pays deductibles and coinsurance?
You may pay a co-payment or coinsurance for covered services. Costs, extra coverage, and rules vary by plan.

Two ways to get drug coverage:

1. *Medicare Prescription Drug Plan (Part D). These plans (sometimes called "PDPs") add drug coverage to Original Medicare, some Medicare Cost Plans, some Medicare Private Fee-for-Service (PFFS) Plans, and Medicare Medical Savings Account (MSA) Plans.*
2. *Medicare Advantage Plan (Part C) (like an HMO or PPO) or other Medicare health plan that offers Medicare prescription drug coverage. You get all of your Medicare Part A (Hospital Insurance) and Medicare Part B (Medical Insurance) coverage, and prescription drug coverage (Part D), through these plans. Medicare Advantage Plans with prescription drug coverage are sometimes called "MA-PDs." You must have Part A and Part B to join a Medicare Advantage Plan.*

Medicare payment questions and answers:

If you have Medicare and other health insurance or coverage, each type of coverage is called a "payer." When there's more than one payer, "coordination of benefits" rules decide which one pays first. The "primary payer" pays what it owes on your bills first, and then sends the rest to the "secondary payer" to pay. In some cases, there may also be a third payer.

What it means to pay primary or secondary:

- *The insurance that pays first (primary payer) pays up to the limits of its coverage.*
- *The one that pays second (secondary payer) only pays if there are costs the primary insurer didn't cover.*
- *The secondary payer (which may be Medicare) may not pay all the uncovered costs.*
- *If your employer insurance is the secondary payer, you may need to enroll in Medicare Part B before your insurance will pay.*

Paying "first" means paying the whole bill up to the limits of the coverage. It doesn't always mean the primary payer pays first in time. If the insurance company doesn't pay the claim promptly (usually within 120 days), your doctor or other provider may bill Medicare. Medicare may make a conditional payment to pay the bill, and then later recover any payments the primary payer should've made.

Unless you have Medicare coverage or you work in the healthcare insurance industry or you have been investigating Medicare claims for many years, you've probably scratched (*or banged*) your head a few times trying to figure out all of the above. The complexity makes you wonder how many people over age 65 actually understand it. *Now you understand why I said you must keep reading, learning, and asking questions.*

About Medicaid

The following information was reprinted in June 2015 from Medicare's website (www.medicare.gov).

Medicaid is a joint federal and state program that helps with medical costs for some people with limited income and resources. Medicaid also offers benefits not normally covered by Medicare, like nursing home care and personal care services.

Each state has different rules about eligibility and applying for Medicaid. Call your state Medicaid program to see if you qualify and learn how to apply.

Even if your income exceeds Medicaid income levels in your state, you may be eligible under Medicaid spend down rules. Under the "spend down" process, some states allow

> *you to become eligible for Medicaid as "medically needy," even if you have too much income to qualify. This process allows you to "spend down," or subtract, your medical expenses from your income to become eligible for Medicaid.*
>
> *To be eligible as "medically needy," your measurable resources also have to be under the resource amount allowed in your state. Call your state Medicaid program to see if you qualify and learn how to apply.*
>
> *Some people who are eligible for both Medicare and Medicaid are called "dual eligibles." If you have Medicare and full Medicaid coverage, most of your health care costs are likely covered.*
>
> *You can get your Medicare coverage through Original Medicare or a Medicare Advantage Plan (Part C). If you have Medicare and full Medicaid, you'll get your Part D prescription drugs through Medicare, and you'll automatically qualify for Extra Help paying for your Medicare prescription drug coverage (Part D). Medicaid may still cover some drugs and other care that Medicare doesn't cover.*

Author's Note: *Just by reading the earlier text you can see that fraudulent claims for the same patients could be submitted to both Medicare and Medicaid. When conducting your investigations consider that several other insurance companies and government insurance programs may have also fallen victim to the same schemes involving the same patients and/or the same fraudsters.*

Documents

Although many healthcare claim forms, documents, and related information are completed, submitted, filed, or stored electronically; I still refer to them simply as documents. Much of the financial summary information is also stored as data in programs like Microsoft Excel and Access. As an investigator you might ask, "What healthcare documents, data and information already exist?" Some are listed here.

Documentation about the provider

Very often, the referral you receive will include information about the provider. But sometimes you have to start from scratch.

The Internet, websites, and social media

The Internet can often provide some good leads about providers if you have their names. Many times, you will find news stories, court cases, complaints, and even social media accounts that provide much insight about the provider, which is sometimes posted by the providers themselves! Many healthcare facility websites list the names of all of their providers and staff, and even include photographs.

Author's Notes: *Many providers (especially foreigners) have first or last names that are difficult to spell or pronounce. Sometimes, they intentionally (or unintentionally) vary the spellings of their own names. They might also use their middle names instead of their first names (even many Americans do that). Some providers reverse their first name and their last name. In one case, I found a state medical license in which the provider used his real first name and then I later found a business license where the same individual used his middle name instead of his first. Worse yet, other people in the claim process also often misspell those names when typing. When querying by name, don't always assume you have or are using the correct spelling of that name. Also, make sure that you correctly type each provider's unique NPI number.*

Names of providers at a facility

In law enforcement and in private investigations, a common investigative technique to utilize is surveillance where license plates parked at the facility can be identified and later cross-checked with various databases. Law enforcement has access to more information than private industry. Very often, the names of providers will be listed right on the front door of the facility. That information is also often listed on the provider's website.

Insurance companies and government healthcare insurance programs

Insurance companies and government programs that accept insurance claims from a provider should have files and detailed information about that provider and the provider's patients. The provider's file may contain almost a complete background on the individual (and/or practice) and probably includes a signed provider network agreement, which often reflects that the provider certified that he or she will follow that insurance company's (government program's) claims submission procedures and stay abreast of any changes when filing any claims for payment. That provider certification document can be valuable to your investigation because if that's what it says, the provider really doesn't have a valid excuse when saying they didn't know the rules when submitting the (false) claims.

National Provider Number

The Centers for Medicare and Medicaid Services (CMS) will also have information on the provider since that is where the provider got assigned their National Provider Identifier (NPI). Depending on the investigator's authority, the information may not be releasable.

DEA Number

U.S. healthcare providers that prescribe controlled substances must also obtain a Drug Enforcement Administration Registration Number, commonly referred to as a DEA Number. Examples of those who must obtain DEA Numbers include medical practitioners, dentists, and even veterinarians. The DEA Number is used to track controlled substances and is often used as a unique "prescriber number."

The following was reprinted from the DEA's website in June 2015: "DEA does not release physician registration information (or other registrants) to the general public. The best way for the public to ascertain a physician's status is to check with a state's medical board. Registration validation is available to current DEA registrants at www.deadiversion.usdoj.gov." (http://www.justice.gov/dea/resource-center/how-do-i.shtml).

State medical licensing boards

State medical licensing boards will have information on the provider, and sometimes some of that information is available for review by the general public over the Internet.

Business and corporate licensing and filings

As mentioned, some providers also have state, county, city, or local business licenses, and those public records can be searched. Secretary of State record searches will often show if the provider is affiliated as an officer or agent with a corporation. This information can also come in handy when it comes to financial recoveries—especially if you learn they own multiple businesses. Do not forget to also check for any businesses using the provider's home address. Sometimes, the provider's (and/or their spouses) own several entities that are affiliated with their medical practices.

Provider's previous healthcare facilities

If the provider previously worked for other medical facilities, the other facilities will probably still have information about them.

Although the aforementioned list is not all inclusive, you can see there are many different types of information, documents, and records you can obtain on or about healthcare providers. Remember, if you are going to use any of the information obtained for court purposes, get it (legally) from the best and most reliable sources.

Documentation about healthcare facilities

Using some of the same sources listed earlier will often identify the names of all providers that currently or previously worked at the healthcare facility you are interested in. When I served as a federal agent, I always obtained the information directly from the affected government insurance program(s). As a private investigator and consultant, I always check the Internet first, followed by a drive-by of the facility, in addition to checking other subscribed to sources.

Patient and medical documents and records

There are many different types of patient and medical documents or records that exist that will help prove or disprove if fraud occurred, and there are often many different sources where these can be obtained.

This chapter describes the types of records. Chapter 6, "Investigative Sources and Resources," describes where to get these records. Chapter 7, "Investigative Tools and Techniques," describes how to get these documents.

Types of documents and records

- Patient files (including lab and other related files)
- Treatment or service files
- Insurance claim forms
- Proof of payment (or lack of payment)
- Explanation of Benefits (EOB) forms
- Appointment books (for patients)
- Sign-in logs (for patients)
- Employee personnel files
- Provider and healthcare facility files (described earlier)
- E-mails
- Financial records (suspect's bank accounts and other assets)

Author's Notes: *Ambulance, pharmacist, DME and other suppliers, and so forth will also have their own unique records and documents that you may need. Examples might include patient pickup and drop-off logs, doctor prescriptions, shipping, receiving, and delivery records, as well as financial accounts payable and accounts receivable.*

The next chapter is on investigative sources and resources, which also describes where to obtain these documents and records.

chapter six

Investigative sources and resources

Investigative sources

Information that you want and need is often available from more than one source. Of course, some sources might be considered more reliable than others, and some are considered the "most reliable." Don't make the mistake of thinking there is only one place to legally obtain the documentation or information you need. Sometimes, that might be true, but it's not always. Sometimes, investigators have a tendency to think "either or" when they could or should be thinking "both," "many," or "all of the above." Obtaining information from more than one source helps corroborate the information.

WAR STORY 6.1

During a highly complex financial fraud investigation, I relied on an experienced auditor who was also an accountant to review and analyze cost and expense reports. He was very patient and better at that kind of stuff than me. Because of his expertise in accounting, I later asked him to review a list of questions I planned on asking the chief financial officer (CFO) of the suspect company. The auditor reviewed the list and opined that several questions did not need to be asked of the CFO. The auditor said, "We don't need to ask these questions because we already know the answers to them."

What the auditor did not understand was that we were not playing a game of "Who done it." Although it was true that we already knew the answers to the questions, that was immaterial. I was trying to put together a strong case in which information could be corroborated by several different sources. By corroborating the information, I could be confidant that (1) the information was accurate and (2) the suspect's defense attorney would have a more difficult time trying to refute the information. In short, the more sources you obtain the same information from, the more likely the information will be considered credible or reliable.

Locations of documents and records

The following information and most of the investigative information in this book applies to individuals who actually have the authority to conduct healthcare fraud investigations, not the general public. As you know, members of the general public don't always have access to the same sources or information as law enforcement officers and insurance investigators.

Author's Note: *Members of the general public are permitted to make open source and public information requests, Freedom of Information Act (FOIA) Requests, and they can check open court documents and other records as well as perform Internet searches. Their attorneys may be able to issue subpoenas and take additional steps to obtain information. Don't expect quick responses when requesting documents or information from the government and do expect that you may have to pay for the costs of copying, research, and mailing. A private citizen's requests for some information may be denied if the release of that information is not permitted. Sometimes, it's worth appealing denials.*

As mentioned in Chapter 5, the following are the types of documents and records that investigators often need when conducting healthcare provider investigations:

- Patient files (including lab and other related files)
- Treatment/service files
- Insurance claim forms
- Proof of payment (or lack of payment)
- Explanation of Benefits (EOB) forms
- Appointment books (for patients)
- Sign-in logs (for patients)
- Employee personnel files
- Provider and healthcare facility files (described earlier)
- E-mails
- Financial records (suspect bank accounts and other assets)

The following is a list of sources where much of the information mentioned above can often be obtained during healthcare provider fraud investigations. Obviously, an insurance company or government healthcare program won't have the financial records of a suspect provider, but they probably have the provider's direct deposit bank information. (Remember to obtain all such documents in a lawful manner.)

Healthcare facilities

The best source to obtain many of the documents and records listed earlier will be at the healthcare facility where the patients were examined and/or treated or the entity that submitted the claim forms. Of course if you start there, they will know an investigation is taking place, which may or may not be one of your concerns. If a patient was treated at a doctor's office and a hospital, both should have records/documents about the services provided.

Author's Note: *Many healthcare providers that provide services at hospitals are not employees of the hospital. Many sign contracts with the hospital to provide services there.*

Insurance companies and government insurance programs

The best source for obtaining any healthcare claim or related payment information will be from the insurance company(s) or government program(s) responsible for receiving and paying those claims. The insurance company or government program will also be able to provide copies of any pertinent rules, regulations, and policies and procedures that were in effect when the provider submitted claims. If the provider previously agreed in writing to follow all rules when submitting claims, you'll want to be able to prove which rules they violated. Having copies of the provider agreement and the applicable rules that were violated (and the dates those rules were implemented) helps make your case even stronger.

Author's Note: *Because most large-scale healthcare fraud investigations involve claims submitted over several years, make sure any material rule changes were actually in effect when the claims were submitted. For example, a rule change implemented in 2015 may not have pertained to claims submitted in 2014 or before. Rest assured that a good healthcare fraud defense attorney will notice that if you didn't.*

Third-party administrators and fiscal intermediaries

Insurance companies and government programs often utilize other entities to conduct payment reviews and to process reimbursements. Those entities are sometimes called third-party administrators (often referred to as TPAs). They are also sometimes referred to as fiscal intermediaries. The program integrity office of the insurance company or government program will be able to tell you if they use a TPA or fiscal intermediary, where those records are maintained, and how to request the records.

Outsourced claim-filing services

Similarly, the healthcare providers might also outsource their insurance claim billings. If so, the subcontractors should have documents you might be interested in.

Author's Note: *As an investigator, you'll need to ascertain who and where claims forms were/are generated. The claims for payment might be generated at a completely different location than where the services were provided and by a completely different entity. A common defense strategy by healthcare providers when caught or accused of submitting false claims is to blame whoever actually typed and submitted the claim forms. Some providers employ their own in-house coders that determine which codes to list on claim forms. Other providers might outsource this procedure. Rest assured that many providers will throw their own employees and their subcontractors under the bus to try to get themselves off the hook. Sometimes, those providers will be correct; it may be the fault of the coders for listing incorrect information on the claim forms. But sometimes, the coders just do what they are told to do by their employers.*

Collection agencies

Sometimes, healthcare providers or their entities hire collection-type agencies to audit their own claims and payment records to seek funds that have not yet been paid (or are believed to not yet have been paid). Those entities usually receive a percentage of the funds they collect. Those entities/individuals might intentionally or unintentionally submit requests for payments that might have already been paid. Make sure you know who submitted the claims for payment and where they were submitted from.

Author's Note: *Any time you see claim dates that are long after the actual service dates, you should make an attempt to determine if the claims have already been paid because those may be double billings. Those collection agencies might also have documents that are of interest to your investigation.*

Employers

Employers often have healthcare-related documents that may be of interest to investigators (especially in workers' compensation cases or when the employer is self-insured).

Author's Note: *Some self-insured employers and employers who pay for their employee insurance policies or premiums actually lie about the number of employees they have or the types of duties the employees perform in order to pay less money for their insurance premiums. Sometimes, employers cover up accidents or fail to report on-the-job injuries even if it means the employers must pay for the medical costs out of their own company's pockets. If you are starting to wonder who you can trust—join the crowd.*

Law enforcement and program integrity units

An often overlooked source for documents and records are local, state, and federal law enforcement organizations. Your suspect and/or their entities may have been investigated for similar or other offenses in the past. Those organizations have records of their previous investigations even if there no adjudicative action. The program integrity office(s) for the insurance companies and government programs should know whether there were any previous investigations of the suspect(s) involving their programs. In fact, sometimes, the suspects were previously officially warned not to do again what they did before, yet the suspects do it again anyway. That type of documentary evidence can be very valuable if considering prosecution or barring them from your insurance or government program.

Author's Note: *The government program or private insurance company's payment offices or program integrity office should also have the ability to sort and filter the claims and payment data and provide it in a spreadsheet format. An authorized investigator will want to obtain this information in a spreadsheet format before actually asking for copies of all of the paper or electronic claims. As a courtesy, don't ask other people to do work and massive amounts of copying unless you are sure that it's necessary. By the same token, don't wait until the last minute to ask for things you need and then expect everyone to drop what they are doing to assist you.*

By now, you have probably determined that it's in an investigator's best interest to get to know the people who work at the insurance company or government program's program integrity or risk management sections. They can greatly assist you in your investigations, and I'll go so far as to say that very often you cannot do your job effectively without them.

Author's Note: *It's also worth repeating that you don't want to confuse the date of service with the claim date. One date is when the services were provided, and the other is when the claims were submitted. Duplicate (or resubmitted) claims might have submission dates long after the services were actually provided. If the statute of limitations is a consideration, the claim dates will probably be more important to you. Keeping the differences in these two dates in mind will also prove beneficial when describing which records others should provide in response to your subpoenas or when using other investigative tools.*

Patients

Former and current patients (or the policyholders) will often have copies of Explanation of Benefits (EOB) forms and records of payment, including any co-payments made (or not made). They may possess receipts and be able to obtain copies of their cancelled checks or credit card receipts/statements showing that they paid the provider. Patients are often able to remember at least a few things about who provided the services, what services were provided, and when and where they were provided. The patients may have written dates of service in their own calendars. They may also know what did not happen, which could help prove some claims were false.

Employees

Current and former employees of suspect entities sometimes bring documents and records home as evidence of fraud because they didn't or don't want to be wrongly accused or because they hope that an investigator like you would one day show up and ask for them.

Author's Note: *If planning on conducting interviews of current or former patients or employees, consider asking if they have any documents that prove what they say, I've found it's most effective to ask for documentation at the conclusion of the interviews to avoid unnecessary interruptions. If planning on using any of the documents as evidence, don't forget to complete your property/evidence receipts and mark the evidence as your organizational policy dictates. Sometimes, investigators just ask the interviewees not to destroy any of those documents, and then the investigators leave without them. That's a judgment call (that can sometimes backfire). Also note that once you interview current or former patients or employees, there is a good chance they will tell others about the interview, including your suspect(s), even if you ask them not to. Before conducting interviews of former or current employees or asking for or receiving any documents from them, it would be wise to consult your legal counsel because company owners or their corporate counsel may claim you need their attorney's permission before attempting such interviews. Your attorney might also object to obtaining records that were removed from the suspect's place of business. Remember, I'm not offering legal advice in any way, shape, or form. (This is another CYA note.)*

E-mail locations

Previously sent and received e-mails often prove valuable to investigators. E-mails can often be found directly on the suspect's individual computers and servers or perhaps in cloud storage. But don't forget that e-mails are also sent and received by numerous individuals. If e-mails can't be found at the suspect's facility or you just don't want to start there, consider seeking copies of them from others (nonsuspects) who might have received them. Obviously, internal e-mails that discuss the fraud scheme can be extremely valuable to investigators, and once in a while, you might find "the smoking gun," which proves your case.

Financial record locations

Investigators must respect others' legal right to financial privacy. Financial records should be sought, stored, and shared in accordance with existing laws. As a private investigator, I often obtain financial information on individuals and business entities by utilizing various subscribed information brokers and collection-type agencies. Subpoenas are often used by law enforcement to identify bank or other financial institution accounts, bank statements, and other assets. Search warrants often also list financial records as items to be seized. Credit reports that are lawfully obtained often provide good starting points for investigators to identify bank accounts, loans, and other assets.

In fact, when people/entities apply for loans, they tend to list just about all of their assets to ensure the likelihood the loans will be approved. State and county property tax assessor information is often available right over the Internet. Court records (including bankruptcy and divorce cases) often include information about individual's assets. Law enforcement agencies sometimes use mail covers, trash covers, and other tools and techniques in an effort to obtain suspect's financial information or tips to guide them in the right direction. See Chapter 7, "Investigative Tools and Techniques," for additional information.

Others

As previously stated, ambulance, pharmacist, DME and other suppliers, and so forth also have their own unique records and documents. The locations of documents may vary. They will often be located at their own facilities, but don't assume that's always the case.

WAR STORY 6.2

During one of my investigations, the owner of a medical equipment supply company was suspected of paying bribes to a government contracting officer in exchange for awarding contracts to him. The supplier was also suspected of having falsified proofs of U.S. Mail return receipt cards, which the owner said proved he did ship what was ordered. I later found evidence that bribery payments were made by shipping them through an overnight private carrier to the contracting officer's home address. A visit to a U.S. Post Office resulted in my learning that the green in color postal return receipt cards that the owner provided to me to prove he did make the shipments were actually forgeries.

Investigative resources

There are many resources available to help investigators prove whether fraud did or did not occur. Major improvements have been made in software that helps detect and identify possible fraudulent claims. As mentioned previously, law enforcement has access to many resources that others do not have. But private industry usually understands its own insurance programs better than law enforcement. Working together provides the best results. Listed here are just some of the resources available.

Analytics and data mining

There are many companies, investigative analysts, and others that create or utilize software that can identify potential healthcare fraud including things like irregular or questionable billings, prescriptions written or received, patient visits, and so on.

Audits and compliance reviews

The government insurance programs and private insurance companies can officially ask providers for supportive documentation regarding questionable claims. Factually, sometimes, there are administrative errors when claims are submitted. Often questionable billings can be easily cleared up when the provider responds to such requests. Not every questionable billing or series of questionable billings warrants referral for investigation.

WAR STORY 6.3

In one referral I received while working as a federal agent, the government's program integrity office informed me that they identified questionable claims and sent letters to the healthcare provider asking that she provide supportive documentation for about a dozen claims. The provider failed to respond to three separate written requests for documentation from the program integrity office. After I initiated my official investigation, it became apparent why the provider ignored the requests. She was involved in a major fraud operation defrauding at least two government healthcare programs. The investigation resulted in a civil judgment for a high-dollar amount.

Private insurance companies

Private insurance company Special Investigation Units (SIUs) and federal and state law enforcement organizations that investigate healthcare fraud often communicate with each other and share and obtain useful information in furtherance of their investigations of healthcare fraud.

Federal and state investigative agencies

Private insurance companies and federal and state investigative agencies often work closely with other federal investigative agencies in furtherance of their investigations of healthcare providers and others. An example of this might occur when an investigator from a private insurance company reaches out to the FBI to assist in an investigation, and then the FBI contacts HHS-OIG to determine if Medicare was also a victim.

Other professionals

Other professionals also often assist in healthcare fraud investigations including but not limited to

- Nurses and other healthcare professionals
- Program integrity and risk management personnel
- Auditors (internal and external)
- Analysts
- Computer forensic examiners (recover e-mails, other communication, photos, Internet histories, chat and instant messaging, etc.)
- Information technology (IT) personnel
- Certified Public Accountants (CPAs)
- Forensic laboratory personnel (questioned documents, handwriting, etc.)
- Hotline call recipients
- Human resources (HR) personnel
- Certified Fraud Examiners (CFEs)
- Accredited Health Care Fraud Investigators (AHFIs)

WAR STORY 6.4

While conducting a large-scale healthcare fraud investigation, a well-respected professional (I will call her Nancy Numbers) suggested that any healthcare fraud investigator could testify about the validity of using a "statistically valid sample" to quantify the dollar loss of a suspect's false claims. Nancy then explained the mathematical process of how she determined the dollar loss to her agency based on her calculations.

I was totally confused about everything Nancy said, and quite frankly, I had little confidence that her conclusion was 100 percent accurate. Based on her conclusion, I could not personally in good faith even suggest that the suspect committed such a high-dollar amount of fraud or owed that much money.

I suggested to Nancy that since she was not a mathematician or an accountant that she find such a professional to accurately determine the dollar loss so that their testimony could be offered in court if necessary. Nancy insisted that I could personally testify to her findings. I snickered and told Nancy that the suspect's defense attorney would "skin me alive" if I tried to testify to such findings. The moral of the story is don't pretend to be an expert about things that you are not. Get the right person(s) for the right job—especially if you plan on pursuing legal action.

WAR STORY 6.5

During one investigation, I pulled 20 patient files and compared them with the insurance claim forms and found false claims in 18 patient files. Based on my preliminary findings, I suspected I would find huge amounts of fraud when looking at additional patient files and claim forms. Well, I did not. It just so happened that those 18 files I reviewed were the only instances of fraud to be found.

There are numerous other healthcare professionals with related certifications that may be able to assist during your investigation. Certifications are available in billing codes, information and management specialists, facility managers, healthcare interpreters, compliance, safety, and others. The program integrity office of the insurance company or government healthcare program integrity unit should be able to provide additional information. It's probably worth mentioning that high-priced law firms that specialize in healthcare fraud defense will have access to other professionals who might try to discredit your investigation. In fairness to the suspect and your own organization, make sure your investigation is conducted thoroughly.

RAT-STATS (statistical software)

The Health and Human Services, Office of Inspector General's website reports that it uses statistical software called "RAT-STATS." The following information in italics was reprinted from HHS-OIG's website in June 2015:

> *RAT-STATS is a free statistical software package that providers can download to assist in a claims review. The package, created by OIG in the late 1970s, is also the primary statistical tool for OIG's Office of Audit Services.*
>
> *Among other tasks, the software assists the user in selecting random samples and estimating improper payments. We have attempted to make RAT-STATS as user-friendly as possible, keeping in mind the program uses technical statistical terms. OIG does not provide technical support for RAT-STATS.*
>
> *Although OIG does not require the use of RAT-STATS, many providers download the software in their efforts to fulfill the claims review requirements for corporate integrity agreements or provider self-disclosure protocol.*

For additional information, visit: http://oig.hhs.gov/compliance/rat-stats/.

Public records

There are numerous public records and other databases that may provide useful information during healthcare fraud investigations. Some are listed here:

- Government Suspension and Debarment Lists
- Medicare Exclusions List
- Judgments and Uniform Commercial Code Filings
- State Professional License Listings
- State Medical License Filings
- Department of Vital Statistics (birth and death records)
- County Tax Assessor Records
- Secretary of State Business Records
- Federal Bankruptcies
- Marriage and Divorce Filings
- Social Media (publically available information—not accessed by deception)
- Internet and News Media

National Practitioner Data Bank

The National Practitioner Data Bank (NPDB) is a U.S. government program that collects negative information on healthcare providers. It includes information such as medical malpractice payments, adverse clinical privileging actions and adverse professional society memberships, healthcare-related civil judgments and criminal convictions, exclusions from federal or state healthcare programs, and negative findings by state licensing or certification authorities. Although members of the general public cannot access this information, it can (perhaps with some limitations) be accessed by the U.S. Attorney General and other law enforcement, State Medicaid Fraud Units, state agencies that administer state healthcare programs, state licensing and certification authorities, agencies or contractors that administer federal healthcare programs, hospitals, other healthcare entities with formal peer review, and select others.

For additional information, visit: http://www.npdb.hrsa.gov/ or search the Internet using the key words "National Practitioner Data Bank."

Dun & Bradstreet (comprehensive report)

Dun & Bradstreet allows their subscribers to obtain comprehensive reports on entities, which can be very useful in healthcare and other fraud investigations. The information, which is available for a fee, includes but is not limited to providing information on

- Company size
- Years in business
- Financial solvency
- Payment and histories
- Bankruptcy proceedings
- Liens
- Suits
- Uniform Commercial Code (UCC) filings
- Officers and director identification
- Their stocks
- Corporate affiliations
- General banking and financial information
- Total assets and liabilities
- Much more

To view an overview and sample comprehensive report, visit: https://www.dnb.com/product/comsampl.htm.

National Health Care Anti-Fraud Association

The NHCAA provides numerous healthcare antifraud investigative training and information sharing opportunities. Anyone who works in or is considering working in the healthcare antifraud field should become familiar with what the NHCAA has to offer. Its mission statement is "To protect and serve the public interest by increasing awareness and improving the detection, investigation, civil and criminal prosecution and prevention of heal care fraud and abuse." Their website also promotes their partnership with "SmartBrief" to launch "NHCAA SmartBrief" allowing members and nonmembers to receive a complimentary daily e-newsletter containing "the latest health care anti-fraud news and trends from the courts, regulatory agencies, and the states, along with technology advancements and other health care anti-fraud industry developments…" For additional information, visit: www.nhcaa.org.

Association of Certified Fraud Examiners

The ACFE also provides antifraud training in numerous antifraud subject areas including healthcare fraud. The networking opportunities with other antifraud professionals are plentiful. For additional information, visit: www.acfe.com.

Coalition Against Insurance Fraud

The Coalition Against Insurance Fraud is a coalition of member insurance organizations, consumers, government agencies, and others that strive to educate the public and enact legislation to assist in the fight against insurance fraud. Its website alone provides useful statistics, fraud statistics, studies, useful links, fraud prevention tips and guidance, and other useful information. For additional information, visit: www.insurancefraud.org.

National Insurance Crime Bureau

The National Insurance Crime Bureau also provides member organizations with assistance in healthcare fraud investigative efforts. For additional information, visit: www.nicb.org.

Those conducting healthcare fraud investigations may have access to numerous sources and resources. Working together, sharing information and knowledge, and continued training will greatly assist in current and future investigations.

The next chapter will detail investigative tools and techniques that may be utilized when investigating healthcare fraud.

chapter seven

Investigative tools and techniques

Most of us have used various tools to assemble, disassemble, or fix things around the place we call home. (*Truthfully, sometimes I accidently disassemble things that I'm trying to fix, but that's another story.*) Power tools tend to get the most attention especially if they make a lot of noise. But sometimes, the most useful tools are the small ones like a razor blade, a pair of tweezers, or a magnetic wall stud finder. As you probably know, there's no reason to always use the loudest most powerful tool when something quiet and simple will work just as well and perhaps even better. The same is true when conducting investigations. The more tools you have at your disposal and the more experience you have using them will usually make the job much simpler with better results.

I personally think of techniques as how you apply or use the tools. Chapter 10 details investigative case planning, but before we can plan, we must know what investigative tools are available and how to best use them.

The previous chapter mentioned that law enforcement agencies have access to more tools, which are also better than many insurance company investigators (Special Investigative Units) or members of the general public. But if all are working together when investigating fraud, the results can be incredible. Of course, it's worth reminding ourselves that we are only trying to establish and prove the truth.

Tools and techniques

The following is a list of tools and techniques commonly used when conducting healthcare fraud investigations.

Hotlines

One of the best tools used to identify healthcare fraud are hotlines. All or most private and public insurance companies or programs have well publicized telephone and even Internet hotlines in which individuals can choose to provide their names or remain anonymous when reporting suspected fraud. It is always better for the investigator when a complainant's name and contact information are volunteered so that more detailed interviews can be conducted later if necessary.

Informants

Informants can be very useful in investigations and many law enforcement organizations encourage the use of them. An informant that provides tips or works under the control of law enforcement can be a valuable tool.

Computers, hardware and software

The most frequently used tools when conducting fraud investigations are probably computers and their related hardware and software. Many useful books and articles have been written about the use of analytics, data mining, data mapping, and so forth, to detect fraud or assist in investigations. This chapter will only include general descriptions of each.

- *Analytics*: A process of collecting, organizing, and analyzing large sets of data to discover patterns, anomalies, and other useful information.
- *Data mining*: The process of turning raw data into useful information by identifying patterns, trends, or relationships.
- *Data mapping*: The process of creating data element mappings between two distinct data models.

Search warrants

While serving as a federal agent, I participated in the execution of enough white collar crime search warrants to know that a legally executed search warrant can be the most effective tool to obtain evidence of wrongdoing. The only drawbacks are that they take time to plan, request, and execute and usually require a bit of additional manpower. Because so much documentary and electronic data are usually removed from the premises, arrangements must be made to transport the seized items as well as securing them. The chain of custody of items seized must also remain intact. The investigator(s) must later review and examine the items that were seized.

One of the biggest problems often encountered after executing search warrants on healthcare provider fraud cases is that the provider(s) or their attorney(s) will call saying that they need copies of many or most of the documents seized in order to continue treating their patients. Well, you sure as heck can't respond by saying you are too busy to get them copies. And when the investigation is complete, you will be required to return, properly dispose of, or release most of the materials that you seized.

Author's Note: *Experienced law enforcement officers understand to "dot the i's and cross the t's" because the suspect's attorney(s) will most probably attempt to* *find fault with everything the police did during their investigation—especially regarding the search warrant or affidavit used to obtain the search warrant. While at the warrant scene, the police will often shoot video after entering, before searching, and immediately prior to departure. The person using the video camera usually knows not to include audio to avoid "unnecessary" verbiage from being recorded. However, many facilities also have their own internal security cameras that are capable of filming the police performing their duties during the execution of search warrants. They might also have the ability to record audio. In short, when executing search warrants, be conscious of others possible use of cameras and recorders.*

Subpoenas

Criminal and/or civil case subpoenas are often used to obtain documents and records or other tangible items (*subpoena duces tecum*). Some subpoenas can be used to compel testimony (*subpoena ad testificandum*). It's been my experience that documents, information, and testimonies obtained by the use of grand jury subpoenas cannot be used in any civil case. That problem does not exist if the documents were obtained from a search warrant or from the use of an administrative or non-grand jury subpoenas. The information a person provides during an interview without a grand jury subpoena can also be used in both criminal and civil cases. Sometimes, witnesses are reluctant to be interviewed but serving them with a grand jury subpoena for testimony can make the investigator's job a bit easier.

Authorized and civil investigative demands

Authorized investigative demands (often referred to as AIDs), can be issued by the Department of Justice (DOJ) for records when investigating healthcare offenses and False Claims Act cases. These are more commonly known now as civil investigative demands (CIDs). They are essentially the same as civil subpoenas and often used by the FBI, which is part of the DOJ.

Subpoena logs

I've personally conducted investigations in which many grand jury and administrative subpoenas have been utilized on the same case. In one case, over 60 subpoenas were utilized. I've found that creating a log using Microsoft Excel helps keep track of the serving and compliance of each subpoena. It is not unusual for a bank or other entities to request additional time to gather and sometimes copy documents before providing them. Some provide their responses in piecemeal. For example, in a healthcare provider case, the provider might provide all of the patient records for the year 2015 first and then provide for previous years at various increments in the future. Insurance billings might follow later. The investigator must document the progress or risk losing tract and perhaps wrongly assume that the recipients fully complied when in fact they didn't.

Contractual right to review

Often, insurance companies and government programs put in their provider agreements or contracts that the insurance company or government program has the right to review and/or audit any claims and related information and that the provider who accepts assignment into the program(s) will comply and cooperate with such requests. What this means for an investigator is that some documents can be obtained by the insurance company and/or government program without the use of subpoenas or other tools.

One of the advantages of using subpoenas, AIDs, CIDs, or allowing the provider to furnish the requested records to comply with contractual agreements is that the subpoenaed or requested party must provide what you asked for and they usually make copies of everything prior to providing the materials. It has been my experience that most of the time they provide all documents in an organized manner. The disadvantage of using subpoenas AIDs, CIDs, and allowing the provider to furnish the requested documents in compliance with contractual requirements is they have the opportunity to alter and destroy documents or provide less than what is requested.

WAR STORY 7.1

While serving as a rookie federal agent, I attempted to review and make sense out of a bunch of documents inside several boxes that were provided by a business owner in response to a subpoena. (The case was reassigned to me after another agent was transferred.) The suspect owned a medical supply company and was suspected of short-shipping orders to increase his (illegal) profits. The boxes included invoices, shipping documents, bills of lading, payment records, and all kinds of stuff. Every time I looked through the boxes, I got more confused and disillusioned about my ability to serve as a fraud investigator. I later interviewed the company's office manager who told me that after receiving the subpoena, employees worked together to gather all of the requested documents and they stapled each order's paperwork together separately.

The office manager added that the day before they were to provide the subpoenaed documents to my office, the company owner announced, "Unstaple everything and mix up all the documents! My attorney just told me we are required to provide the Feds what they asked for but there is no requirement to keep it organized." The employees reluctantly did what their boss told them to do.

Well, at least I learned why I was having such a difficult time when trying to review those documents. To make the long story short, with the help of witnesses, the company owner was later sentenced to prison for submitting false claims for payment to the government.

Analysis and audits

As mentioned earlier, insurance companies and government healthcare programs often conduct their own periodic audits and have teams of analysts that routinely analyze insurance claims and payments. Although these audits and analysis are usually performed before making referrals for official investigations, they are still valuable tools when it comes to investigating healthcare fraud. Sometimes, they can run additional queries to assist in an investigation after it has been initiated.

Trash covers

Trash covers is a nice sounding name for searching through or taking the trash that your suspect places at the curb for trash pick up. Investigators should check their state and local laws regarding taking or looking through other people's trash cans. When performed legally, however, sometimes strong evidence can be obtained. Many people think once they put documents or other items in the trash, the documents no longer exist. But as identity thieves have proven, the documents still exist and may contain valuable information.

Mail covers

As a federal agent, I often used mail covers on my white collar crime investigations. Essentially, the law enforcement investigator prepares and submits an official request that meets the U.S. Postal Service's guidelines. If approved, the post office will provide a listing of the information listed on the outside of the envelopes or packages delivered to the address (or specified name[s] at the address) to the investigator on a 30-day increment for a specified time period (usually up to 90 days).

The information provided only includes things like the name addressed to, the return address information, and the postmark date, city, and state. The results provided to the investigator cannot be copied and must actually be returned to the designated U.S. Postal Service officials. The information obtained often helps identify the suspect's aliases and the financial institutions they are affiliated with. In healthcare fraud cases, mail covers can assist in identifying insurance companies, government healthcare programs, and others that the provider is doing business with. This is a nice way to identify potential victim entities (especially private insurance companies because there are so many of them). A mail cover can also identify the names of other providers or entities using the same address. I must emphasize that the envelopes are never opened by postal employees and the contents of the mailings are never known by the investigator.

Surveillance

Surveillance of a provider's place of employment, and perhaps of the actual provider, can often result in useful information, good insight, or solid evidence being obtained. The evidence would normally be in the form of photographs or videos. Examples of information that could be obtained are the hours and locations that providers work on specific dates, license plate numbers, the number of people (patients) entering and leaving, and so forth.

Surveillance can also pay big dividends when performed on the person who falsely reports they are unable to work or perform physical activity. As a private investigator, I've performed countless hours of surveillance of such personnel and it's amazing what people are seen doing that they said they couldn't. It's always best to be able to get a video of the person performing the physical activity they said they couldn't two days in a row so they can't say, "Yep, I did it one day just to see if I could. But right after that, I was in so much pain that I had to lie in bed all day and night because I couldn't move."

Author's Note: *Some insurance companies require any video taken to also have the date and time stamped onto the video. You may not know it but some (perhaps all) high-definition video cameras might display the date and time when played on your video camera but may not show it when you download it to your computer. I have contacted other PIs across the United States and many have experienced the same problem. Some found solutions such as first recording the video directly to a DVD recorder (not to their computer) and then copying the DVD onto their computer. In September 2014, I purchased some hardware that comes with its own software that allowed me to download the video to a computer with the date and time stamp. It's called "Dazzle DVD Recorder HD" and* *comes with a CD (software) with Pinnacle Studio for Dazzle. I also had to purchase separately a Sony Handycam AV cable (VMC-15MR2). This combination worked for me and my Sony HD Video Camera. Please do your own research before making any purchases.*

Undercovers

Approved and legally performed undercovers often result in undisputable proof of illegal acts and the suspect's knowledge and intent. Having audio or audio and video proof is very difficult for the suspect or their attorney to overcome. The most obvious defense attempt will be to suggest entrapment by the person(s) working undercover. Often, it's good to get more than one day's worth of evidence to show a clear pattern of illegal activity. An example might be a doctor who wrote prescriptions for controlled pain medication on three different days for three different (undercover) patients who had no need for such medication and perhaps even said they were going to illegally sell the drugs on the street. (*Maybe that last part would be pushing it.*)

Consensual monitored recordings

Witnesses and sometimes suspects can be asked to voluntarily (without coercion) meet with or telephone select other individuals believed to have knowledge and to converse with and record those conversations in an attempt to obtain evidence that may assist in proving or disproving criminal activity or other wrongdoing. Approval is normally granted by the law enforcement agency's high-ranking superiors—often preceded by internal counsel's legal review.

Author's Note: *Law enforcement and others considering the use of recording devices should ensure they are following the letter of the law(s). Non-law enforcement personnel should ensure they follow the laws of the states that both the callers and receivers are in.*

Polygraphs and deception detectors

Investigators should know and abide by any applicable laws before even asking anyone if they would take or consider taking a polygraph (commonly referred to as a lie detector test) or participate in any other deception-detecting examination. That being said, such tools used by trained professionals have been found to be useful in identifying not only liars but also truth tellers, which can eliminate some people from further suspicion.

Websites, social media, and the Internet

Websites

Most providers that own their own healthcare practices or their employers have business websites, which often provide incredible amounts of useful information for investigators. A website may include the names and photographs of providers and other employees, specialty areas, hospital affiliations, hours of operation, and so forth.

Author's Note: *Some online resources allow viewers to search Internet archives of particular websites at no cost, which can assist in identifying previous providers, employees, and other information. At the time of this writing, one such source is called "Internet Archive: Wayback Machine." For additional information, visit: http://archive.org/web/.*

Social media

Many people (including providers and patients) and businesses publicly post useful information and photographs on social media sites like Facebook, Twitter, Pinterest, and LinkedIn. Some also create and post YouTube videos. Because LinkedIn is intended for professional profiles, people often list their current and former employers, where and when they went to school, and sometimes their e-mail addresses and telephone numbers.

It should be noted that at the time of this writing, those with LinkedIn accounts have the ability to see who has viewed their profile unless the person viewing chooses to be anonymous. Check your settings before viewing LinkedIn profiles if that is a concern.

Author's Note: *An attorney recently informed me that while attending a training conference, the instructor said that if an investigator checks or views a represented party's LinkedIn profile, that it could be considered unlawful communication (because they are represented by an attorney). The instructor reasoned that the represented party could see who checked their profile and therefore it was a "communication." Based on this information, you should check with your own legal counsel before making such searches or clicking on someone else's profile (that's my CYA note), and it's probably another reason to make sure your own profile search settings are listed as anonymous.*

As a private investigator, I often check suspect's public information posted on social media sites. I can tell you that some reportedly "injured" people post some telling photos of themselves on social media. Sometimes, their friends post telling photos about them too. Some photos show the suspects physically doing things that they said they couldn't do while smiling brightly for the camera.

The Internet

Simply entering a provider's name and perhaps their medical designation and city and state in your search engine will often identify additional useful information about the provider including their work specialty area, place of employment, hospital affiliations, complaints, and sometimes even lawsuits as a plaintiff or defendant.

Asking

During my 30+ years as an investigator, I've received some of the best information and evidence just by asking for it. People I've interviewed sometimes bring evidence with them and even glance at it during interviews. When the interview is completed, I ask if I can make copies (or have the originals) of those documents. Sometimes, former and even current employees bring home physical proof of wrongdoing because they didn't like what was going on at work. At the conclusion of the interview, I often ask if they have any documents they want to give me. Even providers will sometimes give you documents just because you asked for them. Remember that people have the right to refuse, so don't do or say anything that could be perceived as coercion. Some might suggest that it would also be smart to have them sign something (perhaps a consent form) stating that they provided the documents freely without coercion. You might want to have them initial and date each page that they give you. Some attorneys might even suggest getting documents received notarized.

Others

This listing is not inclusive of all possible investigative tools and techniques available for investigating healthcare providers and others. You can make any pen-and-ink entries here if you so desire.

Author's Note: *You can use as many or as few investigative tools and techniques that are needed to get the job done and you can use two or more simultaneously when you think the timing is right. It doesn't always have to be "one or the other." Sometimes it can be some or all of the above.*

The next chapter will detail my favorite investigative tool: interviews and interrogations (as they pertain to healthcare fraud investigations). The chapter also provides sample questions to ask whistleblowers and complainants, employees and former employees, and actual suspect providers.

chapter eight

Interviews and interrogations

Differences and methods

It's important to understand the difference between an interview and an interrogation. An interview is nonaccusatory. An interrogation is accusatory (directly or indirectly). An example of a direct accusation to a suspect after he or she denies committing a fraud might be, "The investigative facts show that you did commit this fraud." An example of an indirect accusation under the same scenario might be, "Because we conduct extremely thorough investigations, we know the facts before conducting our interviews. I think there's more you'd like to tell me."

Interviews (not interrogations) are conducted of witnesses, complainants, and other who may have information, which will assist in the investigation. Ideally, suspects are initially interviewed before being interrogated. Well-planned and thoroughly conducted interviews are often the keys to success of many investigations. The same is true of interrogations. Therefore, investigators should continually strive to improve their interview and interrogation (I&I) skills. Many seasoned investigators mistakenly assume that they know all they need to know about interviewing because they have done it for so many years. This is kind of like a professional baseball outfielder saying they don't need to take batting practice or shag some fly balls before a game. Why wouldn't you want to perform at your absolute best?

In my opinion, all investigators should spend as much time training on their I&I skills as they do with any other tools or skills they use—including firearms and arrest technique training. However, not all I&I training or refresher training must be conducted formally in a classroom. There are many books and other training materials available to public and private sector investigators and others that will complement classroom training previously completed.

Two great sources for I&I classroom training are available through the following:

1. *John E. Reid & Associates, Inc.* (For more information, visit: www.reid.com)
2. *Wicklander-Zulawski & Associates, Inc.* (For more information, visit: www.w-z.com)

Both also offer I&I certification opportunities and their websites have online stores where helpful books and other training materials (including audio CDs and videos) are available for purchase. I suggest studying both of these methodologies and others. To best improve, you should continually broaden your skills and understand that there may be pros and cons to using any professional interviewing method.

Author's Note: *When making lengthy road trips alone (and sometimes when I'm on long-term surveillances), I sometimes listen to I&I training CDs to brush up on my skills. You might want to give that a try, too. (Yes, I also listen to rock and roll—I'm not completely obsessed with the job or training.)*

I also recommend that you read my book, *Investigator and Fraud Fighter Guidebook: Operation War Stories,** which has a chapter titled, "Interviewing" and includes approximately 15 of my own personal I&I "War Stories," some of which are humorous.

The topics included in that book's chapter include the following:

- Interview and Interrogation
- Rapport
- Listen and Then Talk
- Note Taking
- Corroboration
- Word Choice
- Planning
- Body Language
- Props
- Finish the Job
- Empathy
- Statement Analysis
    - Pronouns
    - Partial Truths Equal Deception
    - Specificity
    - Minimizing
    - Can't Recall
- *Think Plural*
- Interview Notes
- Interview Room Sketches and Photographs

Rather than repeating everything on the subject of interviewing that I wrote in *Investigator and Fraud Fighter Guidebook: Operation War Stories,**

* Piper, Charles E., *Investigator and Fraud Fighter Guidebook: Operation War Stories*, John Wiley & Sons, Hoboken, NJ, 2014. (Copyright 2014, Wiley-VCH Verlag GmbH & Co. KGaA. Reproduced with permission.)

the information that follows will pertain to interviews and interrogations involving healthcare fraud investigations—especially provider fraud investigations.

The importance of developing rapport before conducting interviews cannot be overemphasized. Also, most professional investigative interviewers will probably agree that before conducting an interrogation, the suspect should be interviewed. In other words, don't start off directly or indirectly accusing a suspect of wrongdoing—interview them in a non-accusatory manner first. Also, remember that the interviewee is probably watching and studying you just as closely as you are watching and studying them. Chapter 10, "Investigative Case Planning, Goals, and Strategies," provides guidance on how to strategically plan the order of interviews during the course of your investigations to increase the likelihood of successful conclusions.

Healthcare fraud interviews and interrogations

Interviewing complainants and whistleblowers

One of the first steps to complete during healthcare fraud investigations (on cases that were initiated from a source other than yourself) is to interview whoever initially made the complaint or provided the information or tip.

In street crime investigations, the first interview is most often of the victim. In white collar investigations, the "victim" might be, "the government" or an insurance company that suffered a loss. You really can't interview the government or a company but you should be able to interview those entity representatives that have knowledge of or made the complaint. In short, unless you generated the case yourself or it stemmed from your own proactive investigative efforts, you will want to know, *What's this all about?*

If you received a written referral of any type, even if it's a written summary from someone that took an anonymous hotline complaint, study the heck out of it. If it was an anonymous hotline complaint, interview the person who took the call because they often only fill in the blanks or follow template forms when completing initial reports. Their reports might include other tidbits of information that you'll find useful. Make sure you actually understand what is being alleged and who it is being alleged against.

Author's Note: *Usually, I make a working copy of the written referral (and sometimes the attachments) and use a highlighter and write notes on my working copy. Sometimes, I write questions on my copy or on a separate sheet of paper. Factually, some initial referrals in white collar cases are very difficult to understand because of the complexity—especially during the first read.*

After reading and comprehending the referral or complaint, do as much preliminary research as necessary to be confident enough to ask somewhat intelligent questions about the subject matter. Early in my white collar investigative career, I learned to throw my ego aside and to flaunt my ignorance when trying to learn about the losses, schemes, applicable policies and procedures, and so on, from others (especially from complainants and victims) who want to help me succeed during the investigation. I try not to flaunt my ignorance to suspects (unless it's a ploy). But I've found it's counterproductive to act like you know it all, when you in fact don't, around people that can help educate you if just ask them to.

My best advice on conducting an interview is, after you ask a question—remain silent and listen to the answer. It's surprising how many "interviewers" are too busy thinking about or actually asking their next question instead of listening. Sometimes, interviewers actually cut off or interrupt others who are still providing information. If you want to learn, then you must listen.

When planning your investigations, you should also be thinking about who your potential witnesses are going to be if your case goes to trial. You can't testify to everything. Find out who has the knowledge that can help your case and listen to them.

Author's Note: *Although investigators are usually taught to first obtain the non-suspect interviewee's name, position, employer address, telephone number, and perhaps date of birth and Social Security Number; I've found it best to obtain the contact and identifying information at the conclusion of the interview instead. In my opinion, asking for all of that typical police report–type information at the beginning of an interview puts the friendly interviewee on edge. I find it's better to learn their name, position, and employer's name at the onset and then develop some rapport before asking case-related questions. Just make sure you don't forget to obtain the other identifying and contact information before concluding the interview.*

Time duration and interview settings

High-dollar white collar crime interviews can often last between 1 and 3 hours or more. Therefore, they should be scheduled at times and places where the interviews can best be accomplished. Privacy is paramount and interruptions should be avoided.

Recordings

If you plan on electronically recording interviews, ensure you follow all applicable laws. Some states require both (all) people's consent before recording conversations. You should also consider obtaining written or recorded verbal consent from the interviewee to have the interview recorded. Keep in mind that with today's technology, the interviewee may actually be secretly recording the interview. Because recording devices and/or apps are so readily available, don't be surprised if the interviewee asks you if they too can record the interview after you ask them for permission to record. (They might actually record the interview without asking your permission.)

Many states require law enforcement officers to electronically record interviews conducted with people in custody. States and other agencies may have additional laws or policies concerning electronic recordings of interviews.

On May 12, 2014, the Department of Justice (DOJ) distributed a memorandum to all the United States attorneys, director of the FBI, and other DOJ law enforcement leaders from Drug Enforcement Administration, U.S. Marshals Service, and the Bureau of Alcohol, Tobacco, Firearms, and Explosives. The memorandum describes the DOJ's new policy concerning electronically recording statements. Although some exemptions are outlined in the memorandum, it requires those DOJ members to electronically record in-custody interviews. The policy took effect on July 11, 2014. For additional information, search the Internet or visit: http://archive.azcentral.com/ic/pdf/DOJ-policy-electronic-recording.pdf. Investigators (especially law enforcement) should stay abreast of all policy changes that may affect them and their investigative efforts.

Preparing for the interview

WAR STORY 8.1

As a private investigator and consultant, I was hired to interview a neurologist about possible false healthcare insurance claims submitted. Before planning and scheduling the interview, I spent several hours learning as much as I could about what neurologists actually do, what they bill for, and the actual provider (and his private practice) who was suspected of the fraud. Learning that information in advance allowed me to better prepare for the interview (including formulating my list of questions). It also saved time during the interview.

Most often, I type my interview questions in advance. After putting the questions in the order I want, I number them. One reason that I do this is because it makes it easier to take notes. For example, my notes to interviewee responses might just read, *1. The doctor's office in Memphis, TN,* and if I look at my questions sheet I'll see that the first question I asked was, *Where did the fraud take place?* My list of questions is basically just a guide. I often stray from my list and also ask additional questions that are not on the list. But prior to the conclusion of the interview, I'll look at my list of questions to ensure I asked the questions I intended to or obtained all of the needed information.

Author's Note: *Do not leave your list of questions out in the open for the interviewee to read. Some people are pretty good at reading when papers are upside down too. You do not want the interviewee knowing what the questions will be before you ask them.*

When asking a question, do not ask follow-up questions at the same time. Let the interviewee answer each question separately and then ask a follow-up question. It's suggested that you first let the complainant or whistleblower provide a short overview of their allegations. If you've read their complaint in advance, you might just want to verbally summarize it and ask if that information is correct. An alternative is to let the interviewee present their case in its entirety and then ask questions as the interview progresses.

For healthcare fraud complainant and whistleblowers interviews, I like to try to structure my questions so that they help me understand the complaint. Very often, the interviewee will have professional specialty knowledge and a vocabulary to match it that I need to understand for future interviews. It's better to flaunt your ignorance to complainants instead of later when interviewing others. Future interviewees are likely to form an opinion about your grasp of the subject matter. If you don't understand the case, they may take advantage of that and provide you with less or even inaccurate information.

I'm conscious that this structured interviewing approach could limit the responses to what the complainant or whistleblower wants to tell me. So, after I have a grasp of the subject matter and allegations from their responses, I'll follow up with a question like, *What else have we not discussed that you need to or want to tell me about?* Sometimes, this question *opens a can of worms,* so don't assume that the interview is almost complete when you ask that question—what you've discussed thus far may have only been the tip of the iceberg.

Seven general questions to ask during an interview

As you probably know, when conducting investigations and interviews, you are seeking answers to the following questions:

1. Who?
2. What?

3. When?
4. Where?
5. Why?
6. How?
7. How much?

Additional questions to ask a complainant or whistleblower

The following is a list of questions that will normally need to be asked of a complainant or whistleblower at some point during the interview. It's not an all-inclusive list. The order of the questions can be rearranged as the interviewer deems appropriate. Before asking the following questions, make sure you have properly identified the interviewee and introduced yourself (and your position) and that the interviewee has provided at least a basic description of the wrongdoing. In the following scenario, it's assumed this is a false claims type case.

Author's Note: *Remember not to ask the follow-up questions until the interviewee answers your first question. Ask one question at a time.*

40 specific questions to ask a complainant or whistleblower

A.

1. How do you know about this fraud?
2. When did you first learn about the fraud or possible fraud?
3. How long has it been going on?
4. Is it still going on?
5. Who are the victims?
6. Who suffered the greatest financial loss?
7. What's the estimated dollar loss?
8. Are there any accomplices or others who helped facilitate the fraud? If so, name them and their positions.
9. Did they assist reluctantly, unknowingly, or did they intentionally assist in the known fraud? 9B. Did *you* participate in any way? If so, explain.
10. Are there any patient quality of care concerns?

B.

11. Do you have proof of the wrongdoing? If so, what is it, where is it, how did you get it?
12. Can you get proof? If so, where from and how?

C.

13. Who else knows about the fraud and how do you know this?
14. Who else has proof? What proof do they have and how do you know this?
15. Who else can obtain proof?
16. Where else can proof be obtained?

D.

17. Who else do you think will cooperate in this investigation and why?
18. Who else do you think will not cooperate in this investigation and why?
19. Who else have you discussed this fraud with and when?

E.

20. Have you ever discussed this fraud with the suspect(s)? If so, when and what was said? Was anyone else present during this discussion? (Elaborate on all.)
21. Do you know if the suspect(s) knows what he/she did (or is doing) is illegal or wrong? If so, elaborate.

F.

22. Do current or former employees know about the fraud? If so, what are their names and how do you know that they know about the fraud?
23. Do you have contact with any of the current or former employees outside the office?
24. Do you have or can you get their contact information?

G.

25. Other than what you have already mentioned, how can your complaint be proven?
26. What other evidence exists that can prove the fraud and who committed it?
27. Why (for what reason) do you suspect the fraud was committed?

H.

28. Tell me how the system is supposed to work and how it was compromised so that the fraud could be committed.

29. How could this fraud been prevented?
30. How can this type of fraud be prevented in the future?

I.

31. What happened to the money that was received as a result of the fraud?
32. What types of assets does the suspect own?

J.

33. Why are you providing this information?
34. Why didn't you provide this information earlier?
35. Who did you tell about this interview?
36. Who do you plan on telling about this interview?

K.

37. What else have we not discussed that you need to or want to tell me about?

M.

38. What is the best telephone number to reach you at?
39. Is it okay if I contact you in the future if I have some additional questions?
40. Do you have anything to add?

Toward the conclusion of the interview, ask the interviewee if they have any documents or other proof that they want to provide you with or that they said they would provide during the interview. Also make sure you provide your business card and ask them to contact you if they think of anything else or if they become aware of any activity that might be of interest to the investigation—including any attempts to obstruct or impede it.

As a general rule, I do not tell interviewees who else I have interviewed or intend to interview. Usually, there's no reason to provide that information. If necessary, I can be nonspecific and say that other interviews have been conducted or that its part of my job to conduct other interviews. I don't usually make promises to other interviewees that I'll keep their names and information confidential either. It's my job as an investigator to collect information, not tell others without a need to know who has or has not helped. I let the suspects worry about that.

Questions to ask employees and former employees

I have found that it is much more effective to interview employees and former employees (or independent contractors as the case may be) away from their current place of employment. I usually just show up on the doorstep of their home, dressed like a professional with proper identification in hand. If you call in advance to try to schedule the interview, one of two things (or both) will probably happen: (1) they will say they are too busy or (2) they will almost immediately inform the provider, the provider's employees, or others about the call. In fact, you should almost assume that right after you contact or interview a current employee that they will telephone the provider and some of the provider's employees before you even get back to your car.

If it is accurate to say so, you should probably tell the interviewee right off the bat that they are not suspected of doing anything wrong. That will relieve the heck out of them. Granted, that could change as your investigation progresses but if it is accurate at the time of the interview, you might want to say so.

Author's Note: *Sometimes, the suspect's company or corporation will or already does employ legal counsel who will advise that they represent the company or corporation and all the employees and that no interviews should be attempted of any current or former employees without first coordinating this through the attorney. Generally, the attorney(s) will not know about the investigation until you initiate some step or begin using an investigative tool(s) that allows them to learn of the investigation. The way you plan your investigation is important for a variety of reasons. The following questions for current and former employees assume there is nothing prohibiting you from conducting those interviews. Also, former employees are sometimes more likely to provide information because they are not in fear of losing their jobs.*

The following is a list of questions that may be asked of employees or former employees of the suspect's company or entity during an interview. It's not an all-inclusive list. The order of the questions can be rearranged as the interviewer deems appropriate. Before asking the following questions, make sure you have properly identified the interviewee and introduced yourself (and your position). In the following scenario, it's assumed this is a false claims type case.

50 specific questions to ask employees and former employees

A.

1. Do you now or have you ever worked at ____________ (*suspect's place of business*)?
2. What positions have you served there and when?

3. If you no longer work there, when did you leave and why?
4. Who was or is your immediate supervisor?
5. Do you know why I am asking you these questions?
6. I am asking these questions to determine if you are aware of any fraud or possible fraud that may have occurred at ___________ (*suspect's place of business*). What do you know about any fraud or possible fraud committed there? (Elaborate)

B1. *Ask these questions only if they know about the fraud or possible fraud.*

7. How do you know about this fraud or possible fraud?
8. When did you first learn about the fraud or possible fraud?
9. How long has it been going on?
10. Is it still going on?
11. Who are the victims?
12. Who suffered the greatest financial loss?
13. What's the estimated dollar loss?
14. Are there any accomplices or other who helped facilitate the fraud? If so, name them and their positions.
15. Did they assist reluctantly, unknowingly, or did they intentionally assist in known fraud? Did *you* participate in any way? If so, explain.
16. Are there any patient quality of care concerns?

B2.

17. Do you have proof of the wrongdoing? If so, what is it, where is it, how did you get it?
18. Can you get proof? If so, where from and how?

B3.

19. Who else knows about the fraud and how do you know this?
20. Who else has proof? What proof do they have and how do you know?
21. Who else can obtain proof?
22. Where else can proof be obtained?

B4.

23. Who else do you think will cooperate in this investigation and why?
24. Who else do you think will not cooperate in this investigation and why?
25. Who else have you discussed this fraud with and when?

B5.

26. Have you ever discussed this fraud with ___________ (*the suspect[s]*)? If so, when and what was said? Was anyone else present during this discussion? (Elaborate on all.)
27. Do you know if the suspect(s) knows what he/she did (or is doing) is illegal or wrong? If so, elaborate.

B6.

28. Do current or former employees know about the fraud? If so, what are their names and how do you know that they know about the fraud?
29. Do you have contact with any of the current or former employees outside the office?
30. Do you have or can you get their contact information?

B7.

31. Other than what you have already mentioned, how can what you have told me be proven?
32. What other evidence exists that can prove the fraud and who committed it?
33. Why (for what reason) do you suspect the fraud was committed?

B8.

34. Tell me how the system is supposed to work and how it was compromised so that the fraud could be committed.
35. How could this fraud have been prevented?
36. How can this type of fraud be prevented in the future?

B9.

37. What happened to the money that was received as a result of the fraud?
38. What types of assets does the suspect own?

B10.

39. Why are you providing this information?
40. Why didn't you provide this information earlier?
41. (*If the interview was scheduled*) Who did you tell about this interview?
42. Who do you plan on telling about this interview?

B11.

43. What else have we not discussed that you need or want to tell me about?

B12.

44. What is the best telephone number to reach you at?
45. Is it okay if I contact you in the future if I have some additional questions?
46. Do you have anything to add?

Author's Note: *If the interviewee provides you with names of people that you already interviewed, act like the names are new to you. If you only ask for contact information about people you have not interviewed, the interviewee will logically assume that you've already talked to those others. Interviewees pay close attention to what you write down and what you don't write down.*

C. *Ask these questions only if they say that they do not know about the fraud or possible fraud.*

47. Specifically, I was wondering what you know about ___________ (*the type of fraud that was alleged*). What do you know about that?
48. Are you saying that you are *not* aware of any fraud, possible fraud, or other wrongdoing regarding ___________ (*the type of fraud that was alleged*)?
49. Is it okay if I contact you in the future if I have some additional questions?
50. What is the best telephone number to reach?

Toward the conclusion of the interview (if applicable), ask the interviewee if they have any documents or other proof that they want to provide you with or that they said they would provide during the interview. Also make sure you provide your business card and ask them to contact you if they think of anything else or if they become aware of any activity that might be of interest to the investigation—including any attempts to obstruct or impede it.

You probably noticed that Part C of the aforementioned interview questions specifically asks if the employee or former employee knew or knows of the fraud or possible fraud. If they were involved in the fraud and deny involvement, it makes it more difficult for them to later claim that they were reluctantly involved and only did so out of fear of losing their job. Factually, fraudsters often put their employees in tough positions where they must choose between doing the wrong thing and keeping their jobs or being unemployed. In short, even a denial of any knowledge can be of value to your investigation.

Interviewing supervisors, executives, corporate officers, and business partners

Supervisors, executives, corporate officers, and business partners may or may not know of the fraud. However, they might actually be part of it or the brains behind the scheme(s). If they are not personally involved in the fraud, they will often assist in the investigation. At the same token, they may not want the publicity (media coverage) that often results from such scandals (which often affects the value of their company's stock or future customer or patient counts).

If you plan on interviewing executives and corporate officers, you should almost expect that they will have legal counsel present during the interview. If so, choose your questions and comments carefully and don't give up more information than you intend to. They will probably be fishing for information and before you know it, they might start asking more questions than you.

So, after obtaining the needed information, you might want to excuse yourself, *because you have to attend another meeting*. In fairness, even honest business executives and corporate officers have a right to be cautious and concerned if and when one of their providers or employees commits fraud. Treat them and everyone else you come into contact during your investigation with respect. But that doesn't mean you have to answer every question that anyone asks during an interview that you have scheduled.

Interviewing patients

During a healthcare provider fraud investigation, you will most probably have to interview some patients. Usually, you won't need to interview all of them. Depending on your budget and your organization's policy, you might be able to just interview them by telephone. Sometimes, it's more practical and cost effective to conduct preliminary interviews over the phone, and later conduct in-person interviews for those that warrant it.

However, many people (perhaps most) are skeptical about providing and discussing private information (especially medical information) over the phone where they really don't know that you are who you say you are.

Persons who have been interviewed in person previously usually have no qualms about answering follow-up questions on the telephone. Showing up at their doorstep with a badge and/or credentials usually gives the patient peace of mind that you actually are an investigator. You will have to decide if it's in your best interest to schedule the interview before showing up at the patient's door. While serving as a federal agent, most often, I just showed up on the patient's doorstep at a reasonable hour, when they were likely to be at home.

Author's Note: *Once you contact or interview a patient, they will probably tell others about it. They might even tell your suspect provider or the provider's staff. Therefore, it might be better to interview former patients before interviewing current patients because the former patients are less likely to speak to the provider in the near future.*

It has been my experience that patients are concerned about two things when they visit a provider: (1) getting better (healthy) or relief and (2) their own out-of-pocket expenses. Even if the patient is not directly involved in the fraud, if they are saving money or getting what they want from the provider, they may be less inclined to tell you the truth or the complete truth. Patients may also have concerns that you might target them as suspects if they say they knew or suspected there was fraud being committed. Because of this, don't assume that all patients will tell you all they really know or suspect. This is another reason why developing rapport before conducting the interview is so important. If at all possible, you'll want the patient to like you and perhaps trust you (or at least not dislike you).

When attempting to conduct an interview at a patient's home, there's a good chance that other family members might be present. I've never objected to a spouse sitting in on those interviews. In fact, sometimes I've learned that the spouse was also a patient of the same provider! If and when that happens, you probably elect to interview both. But make sure one is not answering all the questions for the other. You don't want to write in your report that the husband recalled something that the wife actually recalled. If they are elderly patients, they often travel together to medical appointments so you might have two witnesses for the same date(s) of service. Additional information about interviewing the elderly will follow later in this chapter.

When interviewing patients, you don't need to tell them everything about your investigation and what you are investigating. Keep in mind that the provider is innocent unless proven otherwise. While conducting your investigation, you don't want to soil any provider reputations for a variety of reasons.

After showing your identification, you can simply say that you would like to ask them some questions regarding some insurance claims that were submitted. If it is accurate to say so, you should tell them that they are not suspected of doing anything wrong. This way they will immediately know the purpose of the interview and that they are not in any trouble. Things should go smoothly after that.

I usually bring to patient interviews at least some copies of applicable claim forms that I believe are false and I also bring copies of the insurance company or government program's Explanation of Benefit (EOB) forms if I have them. EOBs describe the date of service, type of service, co-payments made (if any), the dollar amount claimed, the amount covered by insurance, and so forth. Sometimes, the patients have their own copies of the same documents. By asking specific questions about specific claims, you should leave the interview knowing whether or not those claims are false or if you have a good witness. You should consider attaching copies to your report any documents shown to the person interviewed just in case you later have to provide specific details about the interview. If you don't attach them to your report, at least include copies with your interview notes. Not being able to recall what document(s) you showed them during the interview would not be a good thing.

At the conclusion of your interview, ask them if they have anything to add. Sometimes, they have lots to add! Sometimes, they know about other fraud that you didn't even know about.

Toward the conclusion of the interview, ask the interviewee if they have any documents or other proof that they want to provide you with or that they said earlier they would provide. If the patient does have their own copies of their claims forms, EOBs, payments made, and so forth, at a minimum ask them not to destroy those documents. Also make sure you provide your business card and ask them to contact you if they think of anything else or if they become aware of any activity that might be of interest to the investigation—including any attempts to obstruct or impede it. Ask them if it's okay for you to contact them again in the future if you have any other questions. That's actually a nice way to get them to commit to be interviewed again in the future.

Interviewing the elderly

I have worked several cases jointly with agents from the Office of Inspector General, Health and Human Services (OIG-HHS) that investigate Medicare fraud. One of their agents told me that sometimes elderly witnesses die of old age before their cases go to trial. Perhaps that's something to consider when putting your cases together. Maybe getting a written or recorded statement could help. In the private sector, some might say that you should have the written statement notarized.

Surprisingly, the great majority of interviews conducted by federal agents are not electronically recorded. In fact, written witness statements are seldom obtained either. Instead, the agents write reports summarizing what was said and keep their interview notes. Now that I've worked in the private sector, I don't understand why the feds aren't required to electronically record most of their interviews.

WAR STORY 8.2

As a new private investigator, one attorney asked me to not only electronically record the interviews he wanted conducted but also obtain written statements from the interviewees. Yet, that same attorney seemed to always work on a shoestring budget. He expected to be billed about 1 hour for a 30-minute interview. The attorney never took into consideration the time it takes to prepare for, schedule, drive to or from, and conduct the interview. Throw in extra time to have the interviewee write a statement and for me to download the electronically recorded interview, copy it to a CD, write an investigative summary report, and deliver everything to the attorney. But I can almost guarantee you that attorney billed his client for every minute of his own time. I learned very quickly to explain the interview process and my billing procedures before accepting such cases.

Elderly patients can sometimes make the best witnesses in healthcare provider fraud cases because many scrutinize everything that costs them money and they are usually more concerned about their health. Many are retired and have more free time, so meticulously file all the paperwork they receive regarding their healthcare and the corresponding claims and payments. Some even keep logs of the dates and mileage when they visit medical providers because it can be a tax deduction. The minds of some elderly people are just as sharp as when they were in their prime. But there are some things you should keep in mind.

As many people age (especially men), their hearing deteriorates. Most need reading glasses and sometimes magnifying glasses to review documents. (*Gee, I think I just realized I'm old.*) They like to talk about other things, especially if they live alone. It's usually best to be careful not to overwhelm them with documents to review and complicated questions. Try to keep it simple. Remember to be polite and express your gratitude for them taking the time to talk to you.

Author's Note: *Usually, after interviewing an elderly person, I walk away with more respect and sometimes sympathy for the elderly. I also gain a greater appreciation for life and how we should enjoy the heck out of it while we can. Okay, enough of that—now let's get back to work.*

Interviewing other witnesses

The types of other witnesses you might interview are endless. If the patient is a juvenile, their parent or guardian should be present during their interview as a witness. The same could be true if a caretaker, relative, or nurse brought the patient to the provider. If the provider works at a hospital on a contractual basis and is not an employee of the hospital, you might have to interview other hospital contractors or even hospital employees. If the provider billed for services while out of state on vacation, you might have to interview employees at the vacation destination. (*No, your boss probably won't let you go to Las Vegas.*) From each of those interviewed, you will want to obtain as much pertinent information as possible. And if tangible evidence is available you should do what is legally permissible to do to obtain it. At least ask them to safeguard it.

In a nutshell, you are trying to establish the truth or facts. If there was wrongdoing committed by the provider, you will want to prove it with as much evidence as possible. Conducting interviews is a great way to establish facts and develop leads. Interviewing the suspect, however, could be more challenging.

Interviewing and interrogating healthcare provider suspects

Before interviewing or interrogating a provider

This chapter led off by saying that an interrogation is accusatory (directly or indirectly). It has also been pointed out that an interview (nonaccusatory) should usually precede the interrogation. The importance of building rapport before starting the interview has also been emphasized. The suspect is most often interviewed at or toward the end of the investigation. The reason for that is you first want to make sure that a crime or violation has most probably occurred and that you've found evidence or identified witnesses that can prove it. If there is no evidence of wrongdoing, you probably have no reason to interrogate the provider, but you can still interview them.

If you already know that the provider is represented by legal counsel, you should request the interview through the legal counsel instead of arranging it through the provider.

Author's Note: *In the real world, investigators don't tell the suspect or their attorney that they would like to conduct, "an interview and interrogation." The word* interrogation *is seldom if ever actually mentioned. Even when summary reports are later written, they usually only reflect that the suspect was interviewed and the word interrogation is seldom included. Not long ago, I read a book on interviewing written by a retired FBI agent in which he described how to conduct interrogations in great detail. But never once in the book was the word interrogation used. I can just about guarantee that all law enforcement officers (especially investigators) completed training titled, "interview and interrogation." But when actually performed, the word interrogate seldom (if ever) appears in any reports. Andy Rooney, the late* 60 Minutes *television* *commentator used to start many of his commentaries by asking, "Did you ever wonder why…"*

If the provider is not known to be represented by legal counsel, you could consider just showing up at the provider's place of employment. Ordinarily, that is not a good idea unless you do so right before the office is about to close. Healthcare providers usually have full schedules of appointments during the day and you can't expect everyone to change their schedules just because you decided to pop in. Also, healthcare providers are known to work a lot of hours. Some also work in shifts. Some work at their office during the day and then at a hospital at night or vice versa.

That being said, it's sometimes a good idea to actually call and schedule the interview in advance. Expect that even if you agree on a time and place that you'll soon receive a call back from their attorney who will ask you a whole bunch of questions like, "Is my client a target? Is my client a suspect? What's this about? Blah, blah, blah."

WAR STORY 8.3

As a senior federal agent, after scheduling an interview of a provider suspect through their attorney, I arrived at the agreed upon location (the provider's place of employment) in Las Vegas, Nevada, at the scheduled time (about 2 in the afternoon). Almost predictably, the provider was still (supposedly) treating patients and I was forced to sit down with the provider's attorney for 45 minutes waiting. The attorney, whose office was in Washington, DC, kept asking questions about the case. I told him I'd explain that when his client arrived. Then, he went on to tell me all the other healthcare fraud investigations that he successfully defended his clients on. Next, he named a bunch of high ranking officials he knew in Washington. Brag, brag, brag. Perhaps in my younger years as an agent, what he said might have intimidated me. But as a veteran agent, I didn't give a darn about his previous cases or who he knew. I just smiled and listened. As an investigator, don't be intimidated by silence. Use it to your advantage and listen. You can always just talk about the sports or weather if you have to kill time.

Before interviewing and interrogating a healthcare provider who is a suspect, you should already know the answers to all or most of the questions you are going to ask. It is extremely important that you prepare for this interview. Depending on the interview technique you are using, many interviewers will agree that you should bring a witness to this interview.

Prior to the interview, you should properly identify yourself (with credentials if you were issued them). If the provider is not in custody, you should remind them that they are not in custody and free to leave or terminate the interview at any time. If you are conducting the interview at the provider's office, instead say that they can terminate the interview or ask you to leave at any time. I usually also add that if they don't like or understand a specific question, they don't have to answer it, or if they want me to, I will rephrase the questions for them. All of this actually helps put the provider more at ease knowing that they have some control during the interview process. In a small way, it helps build rapport. In fact, usually after you tell them all of this, you will see them smile, sit more relaxed in their chair, and exhale a deep breath.

When I served as a federal agent, the policy was that if the suspect was in custody they had to be read their legal rights prior to initiating an interview. If the suspect was not in custody, the suspect did not have to be read their rights before the interview. The only exception was or is with U.S. military personnel. If military personnel are suspected of a crime prior to attempting to conduct an interview, they must read their Article 31 rights under the Uniform Code of Military Justice, even if they are not in custody. You should check with your own legal counsel(s) and any applicable laws prior to conducting interviews and interrogations.

Questions to ask a provider during a false claims investigation:

Part I

1. If conducting a false claims investigation, you should ask the provider to fully explain the entire document and data entry process used from the time a patient arrives at the office through the time when they leave. Also ask how claim forms are generated, coded, completed, and submitted. Ask them to provide the names and positions of all people involved in the process. Specifically, ask what information (documents) is or are referenced or reviewed to complete or generate claim forms.

After that, ask the following:

2. Who reviews the claim forms before they are submitted?
3. Who reviews the claim forms at your facility after they are submitted?
4. Who reviews the EOBs and incoming payments?
5. How do they determine if the correct dollar amount was received?
6. After the claims are submitted, does anyone check or audit to ensure that the information on the claim forms was or is accurate?

7. What exactly are *your* responsibilities throughout this entire process?
8. How long has this process been in use? (*If they say a different process was previously used, ascertain what that process was and when it was used.*)
9. Are there ever any exceptions of deviations from the process you described?

Author's Note: *Specifically, ask about the process that may have been previously described by any witnesses you already interviewed—particularly, former and current employees. During the interview, do not mention the names of anyone interviewed and if possible, don't volunteer that interviews were conducted.*

10. Who is responsible for determining that the information on the claim forms is accurate?
11. What is *your* responsibility to ensure that the information on the claim forms is accurate?
12. When you provide ____________ service (*the service falsely billed*), how do you document it?
13. Who enters the CPT or other codes?
14. Exactly how are these codes determined? (What is it based on? Who determines it?)

Author's Note: *The purpose of asking the aforementioned questions is to lock the provider in (with their own words) about how they say their system works and what role they personally play in it.*

Part II

Author's Note: *In Part II, you will start by speaking in generalities (nonspecific) and move to specific questions. One reason for that is you want to determine what information the provider volunteers and when they volunteer it. This is kind of like gradually turning up the heat.*

15. Do you know of any claims that were submitted for payment that were not accurate?
16. Do you know of any instances when payments were received that were for higher-dollar amounts than services actually provided?
17. Has anyone ever informed you of, or have you ever had any discussions with anyone about any claims that were, or may have been, submitted with inaccurate information?
18. Has anyone ever informed you of, or have you ever had any discussions about any payments received that were in excess of the dollar amount you should have received for the services provided?

19. If claims were submitted with inaccurate information for ____________ service (*the service falsely billed*), whose responsibility would that be?
20. (*If necessary*) Would *you* bear any responsibility for this?
21. If overpayments were received for services, whose responsibility would that be?
22. *(If necessary) Did* you *have any responsibility for this?*
23. I'd like to show you some claim forms that seem to have inaccurate information along with the corresponding EOBs that show the payments were made. (*Show them a few claim forms and EOBs.*) Can you explain how this happened?
24. Who caused or allowed this to happen?
25. Are *you* responsible? (If yes, why? If no, why not?)
26. It appears that approximately ____________ claims, totaling $ ____________ were submitted that contained inaccurate information like the ones I just showed you. What are your thoughts about this?
27. How could this have happened?
28. Did you know about any of this prior to our meeting here today?

Part III

Author's Note: *In Part III, you will be establishing motive, intent, and what they did with the money.*

29. Were these claims generated and submitted with an intent to deceive?
30. Were these claims generated and submitted with an intent to collect more money than you knew was deserved?
31. (*If the provider admits involvement*) Why did you submit false claims?
32. (*If the provider admits involvement*) Did you know submitting the false claims was wrong when you did it?
33. What happened to the money after it was received?
34. Do you still have that money?
35. How do you think this matter should be handled?

Author's Note: *Just ask that last question, and document the answer. Do not suggest options, make any promises, or make any deals. The provider may say they think the money should be repaid. They may say someone should go to jail. They may suggest it's another employee's fault.*

36. (*Optional question*) Do you think someone should be sent to prison for this?

37. Is there anything we have not talked about that you think we should?
38. Is there anything you would like to add?

Author's Note: *You may decide you want the provider to write and sign a statement summarizing key points of the interview and their involvement and so forth. If they take full responsibility, that would be worth noting too. If they say they knew what they did was wrong while they were doing it, that fact should be included in the statement. In the real world, if the provider's attorney is present, it's doubtful you will get a written statement. In fact, if the provider's attorney is there, it's doubtful you will get answers to any of the questions listed in Part III.*

It should be noted that if the provider blames someone else or others or a computer glitch or something else, rather than taking personal responsibility for the false claims, you'll later have the opportunity to try determine if there is any merit to their statement. If the provider was not telling you the truth, which means they just provided their probable defense if the case were to go to trial. By disproving their excuse, you will be more prepared if the case does go to trial. But you are only seeking the truth. How it plays out in court is usually out of your control.

Questions to ask a provider that may have received bribes or kickbacks:

It is assumed that before conducting an interview of a provider that may have received bribes or kickbacks that you actually have evidence of the wrongdoing before conducting the interview. If you are going on a fishing expedition, choose your words carefully.

Just as in Part I, question 1, in the false claims case scenario earlier, you'll want to get the provider to lock themselves in with their own words (box them in). The following is a list of questions that is similar to the one I previously used when interviewing a suspect on a bribery case. That case involved a government contracting officer in Philadelphia, PA, who awarded government contracts to a contractor in Memphis, TN to provide medical supplies. The Memphis contractor paid the government contracting officer thousands of dollars in bribes. Most were in the form of cashier's checks or cash. Before interviewing the contracting officer, I had already found the bribe payments in contracting officer's bank account that was held jointly with his wife.

Part I

1. Do you have any employment besides this job?
2. Are you collecting any disability, pensions, or other income like that?

3. Do you have any investments that you receive periodic payments from?
4. Did you receive any loans from nonfinancial institutions?
5. Where does your spouse (*or joint bank account holder*) work?
6. Are they collecting any disability, pensions, or other income like that?
7. Do they have any investments that they receive periodic payments from?
8. Did they receive any loans from nonfinancial institutions?

Part II

9. (*If the answers don't reflect they had any financial dealings with the bribe or kickback payer*) Can you explain the ____________ dollars that was deposited into your account on ____________ date?
10. (*If more than one payment received*) Can you explain the ____________ dollars that was deposited into your account on ____________ date? (*Continue these questioning a couple more times if more payments were received.*)

Author's Note: *Watch their body language when you ask the aforementioned and following questions. You may even see them starting to sweat. In this case example, my suspect almost passed out.*

Part III

11. Who gave you this money?
12. Why was this money given to you?
13. How was the money provided (*provide details on shipping methods, cars used, identify any personal assets used to transport or provide and receive the money*)?
14. What did you do in exchange or in return for the money?
15. What did you do with the money (*identify any assets purchased or where is the money now*)?

Regardless of the form of the bribe or kickback, with some thought you will be able to develop a similar list of questions that eliminate the provider's probable defense before they have a chance to offer it. In the earlier example, you'd almost expect the suspect to say the money received was a loan or they invested in the company, or they worked part time for the company. By *heading him/her off at the pass*, you took away his/her defense before they had a chance to offer it. Their own responses boxed them in. The information you receive about the current location of assets and what they did with the money could come in handy later if there are asset forfeiture provisions in the criminal or civil statutes used on your case or for other future financial recoveries.

Interview notes

Your interview notes should be saved. If you took my advice and prepared a list of numbered questions for an interviewee, make sure you staple the list of questions to your notes. If you showed interviewees any documents during the interview, you might want to attach copies of those documents to your notes. Many law enforcement policies and procedures mandate that the interviewer initial and date the top and bottom of each page of notes. Typically, at the conclusion of the investigation, the interview notes will be placed in an envelope with the original official case file. However, check and comply with your own organization's policy.

Storage of electronic recordings of interviews

If you have recorded an interview (audio or video), you will need to comply with your organization's policies and procedures for copying or securing such recordings as evidence. My suggestion is that if you think the item might be used in court or that the opposition's counsel might challenge the validity of it or would ask why the original was not secured, then you should secure it as evidence. But you will need to follow your own applicable guidance or instructions on what to do with the recordings if you have them.

Interviewing other healthcare fraudsters

Having read the aforementioned descriptions of conducting interviews and interrogations, you know the importance of preparing for the interviews, privacy, and building rapport. Other fraudster interviews should be conducted in a similar fashion as described earlier. Ideally, you will have already completed the majority of your investigation before interviewing the suspects.

You will probably find that most patients that commit small dollar healthcare fraud will confess relatively easily. In these types of cases, I would encourage you not to conduct suspect interviews solely with the intent of solving, proving, or gaining information about only one case. Instead, I strongly encourage you to, *think plural* because even those small dollar cases can lead you to additional instances of fraud.

For example, if a patient showed a fake insurance card or fake identification card to receive healthcare, there is a strong probability that the same fraudster is involved in other crimes including the manufacturing or sale of other fake IDs for the same and other purposes. That suspect may possibly even be involved in counterfeiting credit cards.

Even if they are not personally involved in other schemes, they probably know who is. I encourage you to plan such interviews accordingly. Keep in mind that the interviewee has no idea how much information you know about them. One thing they do know is that they are in trouble and by using the right approach, the information you obtain during your interview(s) can be very useful and can probably solve or lead you to more wrongdoing.

If your case involves hackers, you should solicit assistance from an appropriate computer forensics or Information Technology (IT) professional to prepare for and perhaps assist in such interviews. Organized crime interviews should be conducted by trained law enforcement personnel for obvious reasons.

Summary

As stated previously, an investigator who conducts interviews should continue to train on a regular basis to improve their interviewing skills. By preparing for and planning for your interview in advance, you will often obtain more and better details. Your goal should be to conduct an extremely thorough and complete investigation in which as many facts as possible can be corroborated by as many witnesses as possible. You should also strive to obtain information that will be useful in identifying other instances of fraud by the same suspect and/or others and also identify ways to improve the system so that future wrongdoing can be prevented or better detected. Don't just try to solve one case at a time. Instead, *think plural.*

The next chapter is on investigative reports and evidence.

chapter nine

Investigative reports and evidence

Investigative reports

Writing detailed summary reports is an important part of the investigative process. However, you'll probably never hear anyone say it's the most fun part. During my 30-year career, I never once heard anyone say, "I can't wait to write my report" or "the reason I became an investigator is to write reports."

When reports should be written and types of reports

Although healthcare investigative reports might be written by following an agency or organization's mandatory guidelines or template outline, it's worth mentioning that there are often several different types of reports to be written during the investigation. Examples may include the following.

Case initiation reports

The case initiation report ordinarily details the who, what, when, and where, and sometimes the why, how, and how much. For example, the report would include the following:

- Where, how, and when the referral or information was received or developed and by whom
- Where the wrongdoing occurred (and/or is occurring)
- Who provided or developed the information
- Who the suspect(s) is or might be
- What the scam or scheme was
- When the incident(s) took place
- Who the victim(s) is
- What the estimated dollar loss is or might be and
- Who the witnesses are or might be

Author's Note: *If supportive documents or data or evidence was provided, these should also be included in the report and perhaps one or more of these documents attached to the report.*

In short, the case initiation report should contain sufficient information that describes the complaint, referral, or the information received or developed. At a minimum, it should provide an overview of the details received or obtained so that anyone who reads the report will have an understanding of why the investigation was initiated.

Author's Note: *Very often, most or all of the information contained in the case initiation will also be used (copied and pasted) in the final investigative summary report. That's another reason for the case initiation to be detailed.*

Interview reports

Anytime an interview (or interrogation) is conducted by an investigator, it should be documented in a report. Perhaps if the interview was electronically recorded (and the recording saved), the report could be written with less detail. But if there is no electronic recording, the report should be a detailed accurate representation of what was communicated during the interview. Sometimes, it's wise to also include information about what transpired or was said just before or after the interview, if it could have investigative value.

Use of investigative tools, sources, and resource reports

If you used investigative tools, sources, or resources during your investigation, they should be documented in a report. For example, if you have performed surveillance, it should be documented and facts included about the time, date, location, and what was observed. If video or photographs were obtained, that should be mentioned and perhaps one or more of the photos or frames should be included in or with the report—especially if they are of evidentiary value.

Another example of when reports should be written would include when you serve subpoenas. If a subpoena was to provide documents or records and they were delivered to you, you should also document when and how they were provided, who provided them, and a description of what was provided. If items were not provided that should have been, also document that fact. This practice will often save you time in the long run because you'll eventually have to prepare an official report summarizing your investigation. When documenting your investigative activity shortly after it's performed becomes your standard practice, you'll always know with certainty when subpoenas were served, when they were complied with and by whom, what was provided, and perhaps what was not provided.

Another reason to document requests and/or receipt of documents and records is because you might find that what was provided contains false information or information that was created with the intent of obstructing or deceiving the investigator. If you document all the details as they occur, you can confidently testify to those facts.

Review or analysis reports

At the conclusion of the review or analysis of documents or data during your investigation, it should be documented. The results of the review (findings) or analysis should also be documented in a report, not just in your working file.

Requests for assistance and related responses reports

Sometimes, formal and informal requests for assistance are made. Reports should document when, how, and to whom the requests were made and what the requests were for. If the requests have deadlines for completion, that should also be documented. The same is true when responses are provided. If the responding party complies but doesn't write a report, you should write your own report describing the compliances. For example, let's say you formerly asked an auditor or analysts to review a bunch of insurance claim forms to determine if there was any evidence of "upcoding." If the auditor or analyst only verbally tells you the review found no evidence of upcoding, either you or they should document that fact.

You might be wondering why you should document it if no evidence of wrongdoing was found. Well, what if you are transferred or the case is transferred to another investigator? If the work and results are not documented, the newly assigned investigator might repeat the activity you have already performed, which wastes valuable time and resources. Keep in mind that major fraud investigations can sometimes take several years to complete. Factually, many federal investigators are transferred or reassigned while working on such cases.

Other reports

There are a variety of other reports that can also be prepared or obtained before the investigation is concluded. This is not intended to be all-inclusive.

Final investigative summary reports

At the conclusion of your investigation, a detailed investigative summary report should be written. Law enforcement and other agencies have their own requirements for this and other reports, which usually also dictate the format the reports are written. Templates and samples often prove very helpful. Very often, information that was included in previously prepared reports can be electronically copied and pasted to the final report. Obviously, copying and pasting can save you time. But your end work product should be comprehensive and contain all the details a reader could want describing all aspects of the investigation.

Author's Note: *The best times to be thinking about the final investigative report are when you write your case initiation and while you are conducting your investigation. Since you know you are going to have to write the final report eventually, make plans for it well in advance and as you are investigating. This advanced planning will save you a lot of time and aggravation.*

Reports and patient information

When writing healthcare fraud investigation reports, patient information and services may need to be included. Check with your organization or attorneys about how best to accomplish this. You may or may not wish to include the patients' full names or other identifying information, and perhaps only include the last four digits of the patients' Social Security Numbers (SSN) instead of their full SSNs. Some investigators create an internal listing of patients' names and assign them unique numbers for case report purposes. Remember that you are also responsible for protecting the patient information you possess during your investigation.

How many reports to write

As a police officer, detective, and federal agent, I most often wrote separate reports for all or most of the occurrences or events listed earlier. However, now that I serve as a private investigator and consultant, my clients are charged by the hour or by the day. Understandably, clients usually want their costs kept to a minimum. To accommodate, I usually write one report and update it as the investigation progresses and when it is concluded. However, if I conduct nonrecorded interviews, I often write separate reports of interview and include them as attachments. Occasionally, other more detailed reports are also included as attachments but they are still referenced in the final report. This obviously saves time (and money). Regardless of how or how often you or your organization decides to write reports, the investigative process should be well documented.

Attachments and exhibits

I only know of one federal investigative agency that does not include attachments to their reports. Apparently, it's their agency's policy not to include attachments. Although I can understand wanting to keep attachments and exhibits to a minimum to save filing space, sometimes reports need attachments.

WAR STORY 9.1

During a joint investigation with a large federal investigative agency, a witness provided us with a one-page document that we considered "the smoking gun." That one document actually proved our case! The assisting agent wrote a report describing the document but did not include a copy of it as an attachment to his report. In fact, a copy of "the smoking gun" document was not even placed in that agent's official case file (at least that's what he told me). Instead, the original was placed in his evidence depository and a copy kept in the agent's "working file."

Author's Note: *If an attachment or exhibit will help the reader(s) understand the case or what was learned or established, the investigator should attach a copy of it to the applicable report. A less useful but possible alternative could be to include a scanned or photographed copy of the document(s) embedded into the narrative portion of the report. But to best prove your case or to share information about your case, you must include (not exclude) essential information.*

Differing opinions about the content of reports

Professional opinions often differ on what information should be included in investigative reports. One federal criminal prosecutor told me to write less in my reports. He said, "The more you write in your reports, the more you have to defend in court." His theory was that the defense attorneys could question things I wrote but couldn't question things I did not write.

WAR STORY 9.2

In one meeting, a senior agent from a highly respected federal investigative agency told me not to include details in an official report that described documents I reviewed that were obtained during our joint investigation. The federal prosecutor agreed with the agent. I asked how any of us would know or remember that the documents were obtained and reviewed and what information they contained if I didn't write a report. I was told to just write an official report reflecting that I received the documents and then to write notes in my "working file" describing what I found during the review.

The senior agent and prosecutor's reasoning was that they did not want the defense counsel to know what we knew. I actually responded by saying something like, "Well, if the defense counsel can get their client off because of something I wrote in my report, then perhaps the client is innocent." That comment did not go over very well and I was accused of not playing like a team member. Frankly, I don't want to be on those types of teams.

In contrast, when working with defense attorneys as a private investigator, one attorney emphasized, "If it's not in the police report, it didn't happen!" Several defense attorneys have suggested to me that if a police officer took the witness stand and said he/she saw or did things that the officer did not previously document in their report, the defense attorneys would be all over the police officer *like stink on crap*. The defense attorneys would argue that if the cop did not document it, it didn't happen.

So, which of these professional attorneys' methodology is correct? In my opinion, the defense attorney's approach makes more sense. Your investigative reports are certainly subject to be scrutinized by the opposition's counsel. But investigative reports should contain accurate descriptions of what transpired during the investigative process. If the accused is found innocent because of factual information, so be it.

Investigator's remarks or comments in reports

While serving as a federal agent, I sometimes included remarks or comments in my reports that were preceded with the words "agent's note" in bold font. My agency permitted this and it was an opportunity for agents to include comment about things like their observations. Each comment or remark was prefaced with the words "agent's note," so the reader would understand that the information that followed was separate from the factual information included in the report. Examples are as followed:

> ***Agent's Note****: The information provided by John Smith during this interview greatly differed from what he said in a previous interview 1 month before.*

> ***Agent's Note****: Based on the analysis of documents, it appears that approximately 12 or more claims submitted by Dr. Jones contained false or inaccurate information.*

You will notice that in the second example, the words "it appears that" and "approximately" were used. In my opinion, both agents' notes helped the reader better understand the importance of certain information obtained and/or the investigator's observations. However, many criminal federal prosecutors insist that agent's notes should not be included in reports. Perhaps this stems from the belief that "The more you write, the more you have to defend in court."

So, who is correct in this scenario? My belief is that it depends what is written in the agent's note. It would be unacceptable for an agent to write, "I think John Smith is guilty." That would really be taking a stance on the suspect's guilt and perhaps indicate that the investigator is no longer capable of being objective in the investigation. An agent's notes or similar comments or remarks should certainly be used sparingly.

Excluding or omitting information

I mention exclusions and omissions to illustrate that there are differing views as to what information should and should not be included in investigative reports. Ironically, when you attend training on report writing, the instructors will most likely tell you to include certain types of information and that there should be no exceptions. Seldom does anyone talk about information that should or should not be excluded from reports. Let me emphasize that information should not be omitted from reports for the purpose of intentionally withholding information to increase the chances that one side will win or one side will lose.

WAR STORY 9.3

As a private investigator and consultant, I was once hired to review a metropolitan police department's incident reports and subsequent internal affairs investigative reports that were written after the incident. The case involved an individual's complaint that he was injured by the police while in custody. My review found the information in the police and internal affairs reports appeared factual.

However, some extremely important information about things that occurred in the presence of the report-authoring police officer was completely omitted. In fact, so much critical information was omitted that it appeared to be a cover-up. In my opinion, one of the police report's omissions appeared to be deliberate. I based my opinion on the fact that the officer's incident report included great detail about trivial things. This demonstrated that officer's superb attention to detail skills and his ability to document his observations. But when important things happened at the scene that led to the injury of the complainant, all of a sudden, the information lacked detail and excluded any mentioning about events before, during, and after the alleged injury. There was no mentioning at all about how the complainant was injured. But it was mentioned that the complainant refused medical attention.

Having written and reviewed thousands of police and investigative reports, it became apparent to me that the officer was trying to protect himself and/or another officer. He was careful not to include any false information in the report. But in my opinion, the omissions appeared deliberate. In short, intentionally omitting important information can sometimes have the same effect as intentionally including false information.

Another source on report writing

My book *Investigator and Fraud Fighter Guidebook, Operation War Stories** has a separate chapter titled "Summary Reports" that includes a useful section on "Common Report-Writing Mistakes," which I learned over the course of my career. I highly recommend that you consider reading it.

In summary, reports serve as historical references of what transpired or was observed during investigations. That's enough reason to ensure your reports are detailed and factual and do not intentionally omit information.

Evidence

Conducting healthcare fraud investigations often results in the collection of tangible evidence or possible evidence that may help prove your case. It's assumed in this writing that you or your organization has established policies and procedures for the legal identification, collection, and safeguarding of such evidence and eventual return, disposal, or destruction of evidence before or after adjudication. It should be emphasized that it is important to establish and maintain the chain of custody of any evidence collected. Needless to say, whenever evidence is collected, a report should be written or this information should be included in some other report.

Common types of evidence collected during healthcare fraud investigations

It's been my experience that investigators in law enforcement and private sector agencies that conduct criminal investigations are more likely to collect and store evidence than private sector investigators who conduct civil

* Piper, Charles E., *Investigator and Fraud Fighter Guidebook: Operation War Stories*, John Wiley & Sons, Hoboken, NJ, 2014. (Copyright 2014, Wiley-VCH Verlag GmbH & Co. KGaA. Reproduced with permission.)

or administrative investigations. Many prefer to just photograph items rather than collecting the originals as evidence.

Common types of items collected as evidence when conducting healthcare provider fraud investigations include any and all of the documents previously described in Chapters 5 and 6 and those in the following list and more. Documentation may be paper copies and/or stored electronically. Those items may include

- Patient files (including treatment, lab testing, dictation notes, or recordings)
- Patient referral records (to or from)
- Patient charts
- Patient transportation documentation
- Appointment files and calendars
- Sign-in logs
- Patient and other insurance billing and payment files
- Explanation of Benefits forms or files
- Financial institution statements and related records
- Accounts payable
- Accounts receivable
- Shipping and receiving records
- Cash payments received
- Leasing and rental agreements
- Written prescription documentation
- Filled prescription documentation
- Medication (***Note:*** *Some medications require storage at specified temperatures*)
- E-mails
- Text messages (and similar)
- Inner office messages
- Phone records
- Company policies and procedures
- Current and former employee personnel files
- Employee payments and paid commissions
- Contractor payments and paid commissions
- Consultant payments and commissions
- Insurance and government program network agreements
- Insurance and government program network correspondence
- Photographs and videos
- Audio-recorded interviews
- Handwritten and/or signed confessions
- Social media and related sites
- Websites
- Other items

As described in Chapter 6, sometimes you may obtain the same type of evidence from more than one source. For example, the provider might have copies of Explanation of Benefits forms but so will the patients and the insurance companies or government programs. Securing documents from several sources usually assures that you will have obtained everything even when one source is missing a few documents here and there. Also, sometimes you may find that one of the entities has an altered or edited version of the same document, which might be a red flag for fraud.

Author's Note: *Once you obtain such information, it's important to safeguard it. Many entities and individuals have gotten into big trouble when Patient Identifying Information was stolen or accessed by others who did not have a need to know.*

The next chapter provides insight and suggested guidance on healthcare fraud investigation case planning, goals, and strategies.

chapter ten

Investigative case planning, goals, and strategies

You have probably heard Benjamin Franklin's famous quote, "If you fail to plan, you are planning to fail." But what should your plans and goals be when conducting a healthcare fraud (or other) investigation? Perhaps you answered by saying, "to learn the truth" or "to establish the facts." Maybe you answered, "to put the dirtbag in jail."

Although all of those answers might be acceptable (*of course, the dirtbag should only go to jail if they are guilty*), let me suggest that you should have much bigger and better plans and goals. You may recall that in the Preface, I stated that this book's objective is not to just put a Band-Aid on the problem of healthcare fraud but to actually try to cure it!

Well, you really can't cure the problem if you are "thinking singular" or just trying to solve or prove one crime or case at a time. To be a highly successful healthcare fraud investigator, you should be "thinking plural" and trying to identify as much fraud, waste, and abuse as possible while maximizing the use of time, tools, resources, techniques, and legally obtained information.

One of my sayings is, "A good investigator can connect the dots, but a great investigator can find the dots to connect."*

Author's Note: *The beginning of this book on conducting healthcare fraud investigations includes a diagram of "The Piper Method of Conducting Thorough and Complete Investigations,"* which outlines how to conduct as many as 10 case-related investigations simultaneously. Using this method has resulted in identifying more wrongdoings by more people even with fewer resources. Some people say, "Don't work harder; work smarter." I suggest that you should strive to do both.*

Listed here are the 10 simultaneous investigations that I suggest can be conducted during any investigation—especially fraud and healthcare fraud investigations.

* Piper, Charles E., *Investigator and Fraud Fighter Guidebook: Operation War Stories,* John Wiley & Sons, Hoboken, NJ, 2014. (Copyright 2014, Wiley-VCH Verlag GmbH & Co. KGaA. Reproduced with permission.)

The Piper Method: *10 simultaneous investigations**

1. Investigating for criminal violations
2. Investigating for civil violations
3. Investigating for administrative violations
4. Investigating to determine if the same suspect committed similar wrongful acts
5. Investigating to determine if the suspect committed other somewhat related wrongful acts
6. Considering whether others might have or might be committing the same types of wrongful acts
7. Considering how others might commit the same or similar acts in the future
8. Investigating for indications of waste or abuse
9. Investigating for indications of systemic weaknesses
10. Considering ways the system can be improved to prevent future occurrences

Author's Note: *Whenever investigating any one individual, the investigator should always be mindful of possible involvement of accomplices, coconspirators, and others who may have assisted before during or after the offense(s).*

How to conduct 10 simultaneous investigations on one case

Listed in the following are brief descriptions on how each of the 10 simultaneous investigations can be conducted on a healthcare provider false claims case.

1. **Investigating for criminal violations**
2. **Investigating for civil violations**

These two investigations can very easily be conducted simultaneously and are often performed by federal and state investigators. It's simply a matter of knowing the criminal and civil statutes that may apply to the investigation that you are conducting and the elements that need to be proven to consider using these statutes for prosecutorial considerations. Of course, it's the criminal and civil prosecutors' responsibility to determine what charges (if any) to bring. By following the guidance mentioned earlier, you certainly can present your case in a manner that best proves your case.

* Piper, Charles E., *Investigator and Fraud Fighter Guidebook: Operation War Stories*, John Wiley & Sons, Hoboken, NJ, 2014. (Copyright 2014, Wiley-VCH Verlag GmbH & Co. KGaA. Reproduced with permission.)

One important factor to consider, however, is the use of federal grand jury subpoenas to obtain documents, records, or testimony. Using grand jury subpoenas on a criminal case can more than just muddy the water if trying to also prove a civil case. Using grand jury subpoenas can make it almost impossible (or at least difficult) for certain information obtained in the criminal case to be used in the civil case. Therefore, the investigator should think long and hard about which tools they have at their disposal and if and when to use them. Ideally, both the criminal and civil prosecutors will simultaneously allow for both the criminal and civil investigation to be conducted in a manner that will result in successful conclusions.

3. Investigating for administrative violations

Many law enforcement investigators and agents are only concerned about getting convictions on criminal cases. Some are also interested in pursuing civil investigations. Not too many are interested in investigating administrative violations. In my opinion, the main reason for this is because many law enforcement officers, their supervisors, their offices, and/or their agencies are often evaluated (directly or indirectly) on making arrest, getting indictments, convictions, and dollar recoveries.

But what should you do if you are investigating and find wrong or improper activity that's not considered a criminal or civil violation, yet contributes to the detriment of the healthcare system (especially the payment system or patient quality of care)? Should you just dismiss it? I don't think so, and I don't think the taxpayers, insurance beneficiaries and companies, government insurance programs, patients, and others think so either.

4. Investigating to determine if the same suspect committed similar wrongful acts

5. Investigating to determine if the suspect committed other somewhat related wrongful acts

It has been my experience that when you identify a fraud scheme performed by a healthcare provider (or any fraudster), the same provider (fraudster) has also committed other or additional healthcare fraud schemes. If you approach your investigation with this mind-set and are actually alert to or on the lookout for additional fraud schemes, you will probably find them. Sometimes, those additional schemes that you identify will be more serious and/or have caused higher-dollar losses than what you were originally investigating.

Author's Note: *Some investigative agencies have internal high-dollar threshold policies that allegations or complaints must meet before they will initiate investigations. An example might be that there must be a loss of at least $50,000 or even*

$1 million before a case is opened. In my opinion, those policies must be extremely flexible and not carved into stone. Too often, good cases are dismissed by willing investigators just because of their agencies' shortsighted policies. A good investigator knows that with further investigative effort, many, or most of those original tips, allegations, or complaints will lead to identifying much more fraud. Just as police departments can't dismiss calls about "shots fired" and say they only investigate homicides, healthcare fraud investigators should not totally dismiss provided information regarding fraud, waste, and abuse just because it doesn't meet a high-dollar threshold.

Regarding healthcare provider fraud, if the provider defrauded your organization, they probably defrauded others utilizing the same exact scheme(s). In my opinion, it is your responsibility to try to determine who those others are. I emphasize the word "try" because in the real world, you can inform other investigative agencies and insurance companies about fraud and/or potential fraud and they just won't react. There's not much you can do about that except to document who you informed, when you informed them, and what you informed them about. Hopefully, at least some of the other investigative agencies or insurance companies will react and join in the investigation if their participation is warranted.

Proving additional criminal or civil wrongdoing makes it less likely that the suspect (or the suspect's attorney) will be able to convince others (a judge or jury) that the fraud that occurred was an accident or attributable to others. It also makes the case more appealing for prosecutors when you identify additional fraud because the harm (dollar loss) will probably be higher.

In short, by proving that the provider committed many instances of fraud and/or different types of fraud (perhaps affecting more than one entity), it will be more difficult for the provider or their attorney(s) to present a plausible defense. You are also more likely to hold the wrongdoer accountable for all or most of their fraud rather than just a small amount of it. If you conduct a less thorough investigation, the fraudster will still have profited from the fraud that you failed to identify.

6. **Considering whether others might have or might be committing the same types of wrongful acts**

Usually, after you have invested considerable amounts of time investigating and proving healthcare fraud schemes that were perpetrated by a provider, you will have developed somewhat of an expertise on (1) the wrongdoing and how it was accomplished and (2) how to investigate it (and perhaps how not to investigate it).

While conducting almost every major fraud investigation, there is a learning curve. By the time you have concluded the investigation that you are working (or probably before), you will become knowledgeable enough to search for and identify others who have committed the same wrongful acts, and you will be capable of completing those investigations in less time. I'll go so far as to say that you would probably be able to make an entire career out of investigating that one case's scheme(s) if there were no limits on where you could investigate.

However, in the real world, most investigators are forced not to follow the trend because of their own supervisor's or agency's direction or an existing heavy caseload. Instead, investigators are often instructed to work entirely brand new cases (or existing cases) and start learning everything from scratch all over again. However, my philosophy is if "there's gold in them thar hills" keep digging!

7. Considering how others might commit the same or similar acts in the future

Based on what you have learned or are learning during your investigation; your insight, wisdom, and foresight may allow you to surmise or speculate that the same scheme (or a variation of it) might happen somewhere else or will happen in the future. Don't dismiss your intuition because you are probably correct. Your goal should also be to try to prevent the fraud from happening and/or prepare for it to happen and take appropriate action.

8. Investigating for indications of waste or abuse

As previously stated, many law enforcement investigators and agents are only concerned about investigating criminal and/or civil violations. Even some of the "most respected" and best-known investigative agencies do not investigate waste and abuse. The sad truth is many of those investigators will identify waste and abuse during their investigations and intentionally dismiss it because they are not required to investigate it or their own agency will not allow them to investigate it.

Consider the following questions while thinking objectively (not like your own agency's policy dictates). If you have learned that the government was paying three times more for something than it should (*Hmm, that does sound familiar, doesn't it?*), shouldn't you try to do something about it? If you have learned that the healthcare system was accidently double paying providers because of a fault in their computer system, shouldn't you address that? If you have learned that your pharmacy was routinely ordering an extraordinary amount of a specific drug, and those drugs were regularly expiring before they could be provided to patients, shouldn't you bring that to someone's attention? (*Yes, you should also think that someone might be receiving kickbacks for ordering so many of those drugs that keep expiring.*)

As far as I am concerned, any investigator or investigative agency that is also not searching for waste and abuse while conducting criminal and/or civil healthcare investigations is not conducting thorough enough investigations. It is unacceptable for knowledge or suspicion of waste and abuse to be dismissed, or *kicked to the curb*, just because it's not a criminal or civil violation. Some might say, "But that's the way we've always done it." My response is, "Exactly, that's why the problems keep getting worse, the taxpayers keep losing money, and insurance premiums and other healthcare expenses keep increasing!"

Author's Note: *If you are conducting this more thorough 10-step approach during your investigation, you will have to ask more questions during your interviews and perhaps conduct some interviews that you would not have otherwise conducted. You may also have to look at additional documents and data. But the return on investment, although difficult to quantify, will be worth it in the long run.*

9. Investigating for indications of systemic weaknesses

While conducting your investigation, you should also be investigating for what caused or allowed the wrong that you are investigating to occur in the first place. There could be deficiencies in management, policies and procedures, security, oversight, checks and balances, and so forth.

Chapter 8, which is on interviewing, includes a couple of suggested interview questions about what caused or allowed the fraud to occur and how it could be prevented. The people you are interviewing who actually work in the field usually know about deficiencies and how improvements can be made. It only takes a minute to ask them. These types of questions should be part of your plan when preparing for interviews.

10. Considering ways the system can be improved to prevent future occurrences

As mentioned earlier, you can acquire good insight on how the system can be improved to prevent future occurrences simply by asking the people in the field. They know and are usually never asked. Based on your own knowledge acquired during the investigation and/or from your own prior experience or training, you too will have ideas on how to fix what's broken or in need of repair. No later than at the conclusion of every investigation, you should prepare written reports describing any and all systemic and/or other weaknesses and/or deficiencies that you've identified during your investigation and then make written recommendations as to how to fix or correct the problem(s).

Think about it. If you could prevent the wrong from reoccurring in the future, wouldn't that be a good thing? Wouldn't we all be better off and the fraudsters worse off?

Drafting investigative plans for investigative efforts

Having outlined the overall most thorough approach to investigating healthcare fraud, attention will now focus on things to consider when developing a plan to investigate an individual provider or individual healthcare entity. Because there are so many possible variables on the types of schemes conducted and people investigating, the following should only be used as a generic guide for consideration.

Author's Note: *Factually, all healthcare fraud investigators and examiners reading this book do not have the same authority, power, jurisdiction, or responsibilities. Therefore, they do not all have access to the same resources, tools, and techniques. Keep in mind, however, that if everyone is working together that becomes less problematic.*

Staying organized

When conducting high-dollar or complex healthcare fraud investigations, you will usually obtain and accumulate large amounts of documents or electronic data. It's important to stay well organized. Consider keeping a log describing what and when you requested items or information; what, when, and if it was obtained; where and from whom you obtained it; and just as importantly, when you reviewed it and where you stored it.

Another reason you must stay organized is because you will probably also be assigned other unrelated cases during this same time frame and therefore might be away from some cases for extended periods. Also, sometimes investigators and agents are reassigned. It would be great if a case transfer could be completed in an orderly fashion rather than handing off or receiving a big mess. In the real world, messy case transfers often result in those cases being closed.

Filing and storing investigative reports

You will recall from Chapter 9, that it is important to be thinking about your final investigative summary report when you first start your investigation. The better you prepare in advance for the final report, the easier it will be to write and the quality will be better, too.

This means that your official investigative case file should contain all original investigative reports written during the course of the investigation. You should ensure that all reports are also provided and saved electronically (*since many are becoming paperless, perhaps that's the only way you file and store reports anyway*). The benefit of having the reports saved electronically is that information can easily be copied and pasted to the final report if necessary and easily electronically shared with others.

Author's Note: *If you've never worked on a nationwide large-scale investigation before, you might be thinking that the information provided earlier is fairly obvious advice. But if you have other investigators assisting at various locations (perhaps in different states), you've got to set the ground rules from the very beginning. If you don't, it will haunt you when trying to compile all of the information to write the final report.*

Saving and storing interview notes

At the conclusion of the investigation, you must ensure that all interview notes are retained (preferably with the original case file). Make sure that's the rule from the start. Follow (or improve upon) your own organization's policy if needed.

Saving and storing audio and video recordings and photographs

It's my opinion that not all original audio and video recordings and photographs need to be secured as evidence. However, copies should be retained. For example, if you took photographs of a building while on surveillance and nothing happened, I don't think the original photos need to be secured as evidence. (Check with your agency or legal counsel for their policies or opinions.)

However, if you have audio, video, or photographs that you do think will be used as evidence or that the defense might question or want for evidence, you should safeguard them and secure them as evidence. Since most recordings and photographs are digital, saving memory discs in evidence rooms can become costly. Some recording devices do not even use memory discs (like many digital audio recorders). In those cases, many investigators consider the first copy as evidence.

Saving and storing evidence

See the previous section on audio, video, and photograph evidence. You may also have additional electronic evidence (claim forms, e-mails, etc.). You will need to make arrangements to secure those too. Some paper documents might also be considered evidence. Occasionally, in healthcare fraud cases, you will obtain and secure other tangible items as evidence. In one case I worked, a patient possessed syringes filled with antigens that he received from an allergy doctor we were investigating. The patient had them stored in his refrigerator. In that case, the syringes were considered evidence and also had to be secured and refrigerated.

Investigating pharmacy cases can also result in the need to secure pills and other medication as evidence. Law enforcement agencies already have manuals and strict policies and procedures on evidence, so I'm not going to try to condense it all in one paragraph. As you plan your investigation, think about what evidence might exist, where and how it might be legally obtained, and what you are going to do with it when you get it. Make sure you keep chain-of-custody logs on your evidence.

Proactive and reactive investigations

Proactive investigations

Analysis and data mining

Many healthcare insurance companies, government insurance programs, and other business entities take proactive steps in an attempt to detect fraud with the use of computer analytics, data mining, professional analysis, or other methods. These are great ways to identify potential fraud. The next step for many is to conduct their own preliminary investigation or inquiries, often without conducting any interviews or using typical investigative tools or methods. Frequently, their objective is to determine if there is probable fraud or just accidental mistakes. Some law enforcement investigative agencies also do the same to identify possible fraud. In fact, it's been publicized that this proactive type of effort has been instrumental in the success of the Federal HEAT Task Force, which has been making a big dent in fighting Medicare fraud.

The HEAT Task Force

The HEAT Task Force was created in 2009 by the Department of Health and Human Services (HHS) and the Department of Justice (DOJ). The name HEAT is an acronym for Health Care Fraud Prevention and Enforcement Action Team, which is directed by the HHS Secretary and Attorney General. For additional information, visit: http://www.stopmedicarefraud.gov/aboutfraud/heattaskforce/.

Investigative projects

As a federal agent, I often opened investigative projects with the goal of identifying fraud in specific areas. In healthcare fraud projects, one of the first steps I took was to contact personnel from my government's Program Integrity Office seeking their assistance to provide me with healthcare provider data and/or to conduct specific queries that would help identify potential fraud. This is an example of how an investigator can accomplish the sixth type of simultaneous investigation listed earlier (*considering whether others might have or might be committing the same types of wrongful acts*).

Undercovers

Some law enforcement agencies also perform undercover activity in an attempt to identify fraudsters or obtain the evidence of wrongdoing.

Undercovers can also be utilized as a tool during an existing investigation, not just before.

Reactive investigations

It has been my experience that most investigations are initiated in a reactive manner based on the information received from the earlier proactive types of efforts, hotlines or other complaints, and so forth. Sometimes, the assigned investigator knows nothing at all about the case until it is assigned to them.

Developing investigative plans and strategies

It is good to have a list handy of all of the investigative tools, resources, and techniques that are at your disposal which you could use during any of your investigations. If you are not a law enforcement investigator, you might also want to have a sublisting of the tools, resources, and techniques that law enforcement has that you do not. In fact, you could also have a listing of the tools, resources, and techniques that other investigative agencies have that you often work with (or could work with). Many of those tools, resources, and techniques are listed in Chapters 6 and 7.

Factually, some organizations have bigger budgets and more resources than others. I know for a fact that one of the best-known federal criminal investigative agencies has many more resources to investigate healthcare fraud, even though they do not also investigate waste or abuse or try to identify systemic weaknesses or other deficiencies, and they are under no obligation to make recommendations for improvement.

Author's Note: *Politics aside, it's a good idea for all investigators of healthcare fraud to know and become acquainted with each other's abilities and resources and their willingness to assist in investigations so that all efforts can be maximized and investigative costs kept to a minimal.*

Investigative planning steps to consider

Here are some steps to consider when drafting your investigative plan and strategy. Realize that the plan will need to be updated as your investigation progresses because of the new information developed and for a variety of other reasons.

1. After grasping the information in the allegations or complaint received, determine if you have answers (or partial answers) to the seven questions: who, what, when, where, how, why, and how much. You'll probably be able to quickly obtain additional information on the known suspect(s) if working on a provider fraud case.

2. Consider what criminal and/or civil statutes may have been violated.
3. Consider where the case can be (or should be) prosecuted: federal or state (and which federal district and/or state), criminal and/or civil.
4. Consider what other insurance companies, government insurance programs, or others may have been victimized by the same suspect(s) using the same schemes.
5. Consider what tangible evidence you know or believe should or could exist.
6. Consider who should or might possess information that will assist in the investigation. Think about witnesses and then think about which of them may be cooperative or uncooperative and would probably tell or not tell the suspect(s) of your investigation.
7. Consider what sources and resources are available to assist in your investigation.
8. Consider what investigative tools and techniques will be (or could be) at your disposal.
9. Consider your existing work and personal calendars and existing caseload and how your time can be best used to conduct and complete this investigation.
10. Consider the best order to utilize the sources, resources, tools, and techniques that will provide the most benefit in the most time-efficient and cost-effective manner without jeopardizing the results of the investigation and/or any of your (and/or others) existing investigations. Also, take into consideration any of your other personal and professional commitments.

As stated, your plan is probably going to change. Do not lock yourself into a course of action as if it's written in stone. You will update your plan and strategy as the investigation progresses. Most investigators maintain a working file in addition to an official file. Your investigative plan should be maintained in your working file.

Having written investigative plans on all of your open investigations will enable you to stay intimately familiar with all of your cases at any one given time. In all probability, you won't be able to work on one or more cases for a significant amount of time. Drafting a well-thought-out plan will serve as your roadmap in successfully completing the investigation, regardless of when you are working on the case.

In addition, should the case be transferred to another investigator, your updated well-thought-out plan combined with your previous written reports will greatly assist whoever takes over the case and should allow for a smooth transition.

Your supervisors will probably also ask you to provide periodic briefings on your cases, and you will probably be required to type periodic case summaries. By having a written plan (and your case reports), you can easily provide the information describing what you have done, as well as what and when you plan on doing other things.

Murphy's Law

Murphy's Law is, *whatever can go wrong will go wrong*. This happens a lot during investigations. Examples might be:

- You travel to conduct an unscheduled interview of a key former employee and they are not home; or worse yet, they went on vacation.
- You plan on conducting surveillance and the video camera battery dies.
- You plan on conducting a suspect interview with another federal agent, and the assisting agent calls you moments before and says they can't make it.
- You plan on reviewing recently received documents, and your supervisor assigns you two new cases.

Knowing about Murphy's Law in advance allows you to make or consider contingency plans to avoid disaster. Sometimes, all you can do is postpone or delay your original plans. It's usually not the end of the world. Just remember, investigations never go as smoothly as you think they will. President Dwight Eisenhower once said, "Farming looks mighty easy when your plow is a pencil and you're a thousand miles from the corn field."

Timing is everything

Sometimes, many steps in your investigative plan can be in progress at the same time. It doesn't always have to be, "First I'll do this and then I'll do that." A good example of this is when agents execute search warrants or serve subpoenas. You can also often conduct interviews (even if they are just preliminary interviews) while you are there.

I often used a tactic as a federal agent when I was going to serve a grand jury subpoena. I'd interview individuals before letting them know about the subpoena. After the interview was completed, I'd hand them the grand jury subpoena that they did not realize I was going to serve them with. This way, the information I obtained prior to serving the subpoena was not considered grand jury material. Some might argue that if I handed the grand jury subpoena to the individual first and then asked that same individual questions, the information I obtained would be considered secret grand jury material.

Another advantage to this approach was that if the subpoena was for testimony, I will have already documented what they told me in person before they were scheduled to appear at the grand jury. This information can be useful to prepare the questions that will later be asked of the person when they appear before the grand jury. I could also use the information I obtained in my interview in the civil case or for administrative purposes, whereas if I did not interview them first, I'd have to wait to hear their responses when they testified and then the results would be considered grand jury material.

WAR STORY 10.1

A fellow senior agent in one of my offices often tasked other agents to assist in conducting interviews during the evening hours of employees of a suspect company. He arranged for each of us to simultaneously knock on the doors of different employees' houses and ask them questions about fraud that may have occurred at their workplace. Some agents complained that a particular agent was making us do his work for him. There was some truth to that.

But the senior agent knew that as soon as one employee was interviewed, that employee would most probably tell their supervisor, which would trigger a call to the company's legal counsel. The company's legal counsel would in all probability immediately call the case agent and tell them that the attorney represented the company and all employees and that no further employee interviews should be conducted without the approval of the legal counsel.

By having many interviews conducted simultaneously before the company (or their attorney) became aware of any investigation, the case agent increased the likelihood of obtaining useful information for the investigation before the attorney could close that door.

Author's Note: *Consider what effect the timing on your use of investigative tools will have on your investigation before initiating or using that tool.*

A sample investigative plan

Listed here is a sample law enforcement investigative plan after receiving a referral on a healthcare provider fraud case.

Author's Note: *Whenever possible, report writing should take place shortly after each step is completed or when most practical.*

1. Interview the complainant.
2. Obtain or request records, documents, and information from public sources and your government program, insurance company and/or third-party administrators.

3. Review and analyze all information obtained thus far (at least start the process).
4. Perform surveillance.
5. Request a mail cover and perhaps perform a trash cover.
6. Conduct simultaneous interviews of current employees.
7. If permissible, interview former employees.
8. Serve subpoenas for records or testimony.
9. Interview patients and former patients and other witnesses.
10. Review all information obtained thus far and prepare for suspect interview.
11. Interview suspect.
12. Ensure all subpoenas and other requests have been complied with and follow up as needed.
13. Prepare for case presentation(s) to prosecutor(s).
14. Brief prosecutor(s).
15. Complete anything else that's needed.

Summary

This chapter described the importance of making plans to achieve investigative goals and emphasized that investigations should be conducted thoroughly to identify all fraud, waste, and abuse involving as many suspects as possible while pursuing criminal and civil violations and identifying systemic weaknesses and other deficiencies and making recommendations for improvement. Sorry, I forgot to include leap tall buildings in a single bound and bend steel with your bare hands.

Can you really do all of this in all of your investigations? Perhaps not always. But I think you will agree that most of us can strive to do much more than we have been doing. We can easily identify more wrongdoing by the same suspects that we are already investigating, and we can certainly try to figure out how to prevent fraud and also make recommendations to try to fix known or potential problems.

Football teams have lots of plays in their playbooks, which they first study and then practice. Not every play is used during every game. But the players need to be knowledgeable about the plays they can execute so that those plays can be called into action with a moment's notice. Similarly, healthcare fraud investigators should approach each investigation with a plan and know what their capabilities and goals are. In football, the goal is not to just make first downs and touchdowns. The goal is to win. So should the goal be to defeat healthcare fraudsters in an ethical manner.

The next chapter is on case presentations and testifying.

chapter eleven

Case presentations and testifying

While serving as a private investigator and consultant, I often receive telephone calls from individuals needing investigative assistance. Many callers have never had to relate case facts to others and they tend to ramble on and on before getting to the point. I understand that many callers are nervous and some don't have any idea what they really want. By asking questions, I can eventually draw out sufficient information to make sense of what happened, what they know or suspect, or what their goals are. My point is that it takes practice to effectively communicate to others information about possible wrongdoing.

While attending federal, state, and military investigative academies, I received training on courtroom testifying. In fact, one academy actually videotaped each student separately testifying in mock trials and then showed each student's video in front of the class to be critiqued by the instructors and fellow students. This type of training is very beneficial. We all learned from each others' strengths and weaknesses. I've also testified at numerous adjudicative hearings across the United States.

However, during my 30-year law enforcement career, I never received formal training on how to present case facts about a completed investigation to an attorney, supervisor, or others. Perhaps it was assumed that if you could conduct an investigation, write reports, and testify, then you should be able to verbally present case facts to others. When presenting simple street crime cases (burglaries, robberies, assaults), that's probably a valid assumption. However, presenting the facts about a major fraud case to others who have no previous knowledge about the case should not be taken lightly. It not only takes preparation but often some creativity.

Different briefings for different folks

The type of presentation you provide as well as what information to share will depend on who you are briefing and the purpose. Your second- and third-line supervisors may only want to know what type of case you are working, the statutes violations, who and where the suspects are, the estimated dollar loss, and when you'll be finished with the case. Higher ranking superiors are often more interested in learning the results not the details. Of course, some senior leaders might demand much more details and question your every move or perhaps offer valuable (or not so valuable) input.

Providing quality briefings

WAR STORY 11.1

When I was a relatively new federal agent and briefing federal prosecutors, my case briefings contained factual information that essentially detailed how I first got the case, what I did, and the most recent happenings. One day, a federal prosecutor who I successfully worked cases with before immediately interjected with a smile before I started talking, "Is this going to be one of those briefings where I don't find out what the case is all about until the end of your story?"

Because we got along so well, we both laughed. The prosecutor knew that I did good work but apparently I got long-winded and took too long to get to the point. As time passed, I improved my fraud case presentation skills. In fact, I often interject some humor while briefing because fraud cases can often be dry with facts and figures.

During the 1980s, I watched a television interview of President Ronald Reagan who was known as, "The great communicator." Reagan was asked how he was able to communicate so effectively. He replied by saying something like, "First, I tell people what I'm going to tell them. Second, I tell them. Third, I tell them what I told them."

Subsequently, I adopted a similar approach when providing written and oral summaries about investigations. Cases are much easier to understand when a brief summary is provided right from the onset, followed by a presentation of the case facts and then providing a brief summary of all the information previously related.

Investigator's voice, appearance, and bearing

We have all sat through presentations provided by monotone speakers that no matter how good the information was, the speakers almost put their audiences to sleep. You definitely don't want to be one of those speakers. Provide some degree of excitement and energy when making your presentation. Be careful not to speak a mile a minute. Just because you can speak fast doesn't mean the information you are providing can be absorbed as quickly. Keep in mind that when you are briefing a prosecutor or law enforcement officer or investigator (and hoping they will consider accepting your case), they are probably thinking about how your case would play out in court and perhaps how you would play out in court. Strive to demonstrate that you are a professional and can communicate information effectively.

Physical appearance and bearing during presentations can also make a difference. You don't always have to wear your Sunday best suit, but don't dress down like you are going to clean out the attic either. It's been said that 50–90 percent of communication is nonverbal. That means that regardless of the great information you are verbally providing, only a small portion of it may actually be received. People might be receiving more information from you by what is not coming out of your mouth. Since that's the case, make sure that you sit or stand up straight and be conscious of your nonverbal communication.

Visual aids

Visual aids are also a form of nonverbal communication. It's said that a picture is worth a thousand words. Studies have also shown that people remember pictures. Therefore, when providing a detailed briefing about a complex healthcare fraud (or other fraud) case, it's in your interest to develop and create some visual aids and/or take some photographs to help illustrate case facts. (*The Appendix of this book includes samples of case presentation visual aids on some healthcare fraud cases.*)

Providing copies of reports and documents

If you believe your case is worthy of acceptance by a prosecutor(s) and/or by a law enforcement agency to further investigate, during your verbal presentation you should provide them with a copy of a summary investigative report that contains much (or all) of the information or documents obtained to date. If you've already completed much or most of the investigation, you'll have to decide how much information and documentation to initially provide.

If it's a solid case, you might want to consider putting the entire case together, tabbed and indexed so that they can take the case and run with it. Alternatively, you could provide a shorter summary report and offer to provide a more detailed report after acceptance. But provide them with some form of a written summary report, which they can refer to in the future. Sometimes, prosecutors and law enforcement agencies can't immediately accept a case but they might be able to accept it later. If they have your report in hand, it will make it much easier for both you and them.

It's been my experience that it's often best not to provide the report until after your verbal briefing unless you will be referring to information or graphics in the report while you are talking. If you hand someone a three-ring binder while you are speaking, they will often start flipping through the pages while you are talking (and not really listening to what you are saying). By the same token, if you hand them a three-ring binder at the conclusion of the briefing and never reference it, they might just toss it in their working files after you leave and never even look at it.

Near the conclusion of the briefing, you could opt to provide copies of your report along with a brief verbal description of what information your report contains. You could also point out where certain information can be found in your report. Your case is more likely to be accepted if you can impress upon your audience that you have a good case that it is well organized and you present it well. However, it should be emphasized that potential dollar loss, harm, existing caseloads, and other factors are also considered before cases are accepted.

Author's Note: *Just like you wouldn't try to sell or trade in your used car before vacuuming and washing it, don't present a case that you want accepted until you have it in good condition.*

Testifying

Days before you are scheduled to testify in court, the prosecuting attorney will probably discuss with you what questions you will be asked. Even if that doesn't happen, if you are a witness for the prosecution, the questions will ordinarily be straightforward and only asked because it's known or assumed that you have the answers. But remember what I just said about nonverbal communication. You have to dress appropriately for a courtroom setting and speak clearly and confidently about your answers. If you don't understand a question, ask that it be repeated or rephrased.

Some say it's best to just answer the question that was asked and not to elaborate unless told to do so. A defense attorney once said that when you are on the stand, "If you are asked do you know what time it is, answer yes. Don't offer the time because that's not what you were asked."

Keep in mind that the defense attorney's job is not the same as the prosecutor's. During cross-examination, expect that the defense attorney might try to twist your words and challenge anything or everything you testified about earlier. Remember that they are just doing their job and are usually very good at it. Try to use the same tone and demeanor when answering questions regardless of who asks them—or at least don't *fly off the deep end* just because you don't like the question or the way it's being asked.

If you will be testifying about facts and figures, make sure you review and verify the accuracy of them before testifying so that you are comfortable and confident about the information before getting on the stand. The better prepared you are, the smoother it will be. But be prepared to be challenged about the accuracy of the information you provide.

The prosecutor will be the one deciding whether any graphics or visual aids will be used in court. It's been my experience that visual aids often help jurors and judges to better understand or grasp the information provided in fraud cases. If you will be testifying about the information contained in the visual aids, triple check to ensure all the information is accurate and that you can confidently testify about that information even if challenged by the opposing counsel.

If you have never testified in court before, it would be great if you could see the courtroom and where you will be sitting in advance. In sporting events, teams usually have a higher winning percentage for home games than they do road games. Granted the cheering fans might help but perhaps it's because they are more comfortable with the playing field and surroundings.

The next chapter will detail post-adjudicative action.

chapter twelve

Post-adjudicate action

Watching guilty suspects receiving prison sentences, witnessing financial judgments being imposed, and submitting press releases about the successful adjudicative action on your healthcare fraud case does not conclude the investigator's work. There are many things that must be done and should be considered once the adjudicative action is completed against an individual or entity. In fact, at the time the case is officially opened, the investigator should actually start thinking about what they should or will do after the investigation is completed.

Media coverage alone that publicizes guilty verdicts, fines, fees, and judgments does not prevent the same type of criminal activity from reoccurring in the future. If it did, there would be no crime today and the jails would be less crowded. Although publicity about the adjudicative action can be beneficial (usually more so to the prosecutors and investigators), it is not the end-all solution to preventing criminal activity.

Fraud vulnerability and deficiency reports

As stated in the Preface, "The objective of this book is not to just put a Band-Aid on the problem of healthcare fraud but to actually try to cure it!"

Every federal and state law enforcement investigator and agency, as well as investigators and their organizations in the private sector, that investigates healthcare fraud has (or should have) an obligation to also search for systemic weaknesses and deficiencies (and possible weaknesses and deficiencies) that caused or may have caused or contributed to any fraud, waste, and abuse (not just fraud) and to document their findings.

This responsibility actually takes very little additional time. Although it may pain some investigative agencies' ears to hear, taxpayers' and other sources' funds should not continually be directed to fund the growth of investigative agencies and organizations to catch criminals when the money could more appropriately be used to try to prevent, detect, and deter such wrongdoings from reoccurring or occurring in the first place.

All healthcare fraud investigators should also be required to include in their final investigative reports whether they identified any systemic weaknesses (or possible systemic weaknesses), deficiencies, or indications of waste or abuse during their investigation and indicate if they made any recommendations for improvement. Copies of those deficiency reports and recommendations should be included in the official investigative case file and should include a listing of all those who were on distribution.

It is paramount that the investigator's deficiency reports and recommendations be provided to responsible personnel (decision makers) of the victim's agency(s) so that those individuals can become aware of the problems and possible solutions and be held accountable for making improvements to reduce the probability that the wrongdoing will occur again in the future. The investigator's documentation and appropriate distribution will make it impossible for those in responsible positions to later say they were unaware of such deficiencies.

The importance of recognition and rewards

Investigators, examiners, and others should be officially recognized and rewarded when they identify such weaknesses, deficiencies, waste, or abuse—especially when they make useful recommendations for improvement and those recommendations (or parts thereof) are implemented. If there is no incentive for the investigators and others to do this type of work, it will not get done. Consequently, the wrongdoing will continue and funds will continue to be lost to fraud, waste, and abuse, and additional funds will have to be spent to conduct investigations that could have been saved or better spent.

Storing and archiving investigative case files

Investigative agencies and organizations have their own policies and procedures regarding how to retire a closed investigation case file. As previously stated, it's recommended that all interview notes be placed in the official file before it's placed in archives. Remember that sometimes cases are appealed and even retried. When cases are "unsolved" or no adjudicative action is taken or considered, sometimes information or evidence is later obtained that could help prove the wrongdoing that couldn't be proven before.

During my 35+ years of conducting investigations, I've often pulled old closed case files to obtain useful information and sometimes to solve old cases. So, don't assume that once your case file is placed in storage that it's in its final resting place. If the case file is well documented and well organized during the investigation and at closing, all that hard work may also be very useful in the future.

Suspensions and debarments

The equivalent of a financial death sentence for many individual healthcare providers and entities is to be banned from or excluded from government programs such as Medicare, Medicaid, TRICARE, or the Federal

Employees Health Benefits Program (FEHBP). These forms of exclusion are often temporary (called suspensions) or permanent (debarments). Typically, when excluded from one government program, they are often (perhaps always) automatically excluded from others as well.

The Federal Office of Personnel Management's (OPM) Office of Inspector General (OIG) website describes the Federal Employees Health Benefits Program (FEHBP) sanctions. The following information was reprinted from the Office of Personnel Management—Office of Inspector General's website in June 2015.

> *The Office of Personnel Management (OPM) shall debar health care providers from participating in the Federal Employees Health Benefits Program (FEHBP) under the following statutory and regulatory authorities. The OPM's Office of the Inspector General (OIG) operates these authorities under delegation from the OPM Director.*
>
> - *Federal Employees Health Care Protection Act of 1998;*
> - *Government-wide Nonprocurement Debarment and Suspension Common Rule;*
> - *Title 5, Code of Federal Regulations, Part 890, Subpart J (5 CFR 890); and*
> - *Title 5 of the U.S. Code, Part III, Subpart G, Chapter 89 (5 USC 8902a).*
>
> *The OPM OIG Administrative Sanctions Group suspends and debars health care providers from the FEHBP, who have, among other things:*
>
> - *lost professional licenses;*
> - *been convicted of a crime related to delivery of or payment for health care services;*
> - *violated provisions of a Federal program; or*
> - *been debarred by another Federal agency.*
>
> *Debarring or suspending these providers protects the integrity of the FEHBP as well as the health care interests of FEHBP participants. These sanctions assure that FEHBP funds will not be paid, either directly or indirectly, to such providers. FEHBP participants may obtain services from debarred providers, but the FEHBP will not reimburse the participant for the program share of the costs. If an FEHBP participant, however, obtains such services in good faith and without knowledge that the provider had been sanctioned, their costs may be covered.*

> *The names of health care providers who have been sanctioned by our office are made available to FEHBP Health Insurance Carriers through the secure OPM Debar Webpage. The list of sanctioned providers is also available to the public through the General Services Administration's governmentwide list of exclusions known as the System for Award Management or SAM (www.sam.gov), formerly the Excluded Parties List System (EPLS).*
>
> *As a member of the Interagency Suspension and Debarment Committee (ISDC), we are dedicated to working with other Executive Branch organizations to provide support for Governmentwide suspension and debarment programs.*

For additional details, visit OPM OIG's website: http://www.opm.gov/our-inspector-general/fehbp-administrative-sanctions/.

Providers who are suspected of criminal or civil false claims (and the attorneys that represent them) know that being suspended or debarred essentially means "game over." Therefore, they often attempt to negotiate settlements in which the providers agree to reimburse losses and perhaps pay fines and/or the cost of investigation as long as they are not excluded from government programs. Sometimes, the government prosecutors and investigators don't really want to see the suspect provider(s) go out of business because if that happens, the provider(s) may not be able to repay the losses and fines.

During my federal law enforcement career investigating healthcare fraud, I found that it's not unusual for a healthcare provider suspected of having committing fraud to plead guilty to a misdemeanor or Internal Revenue Service violation or agree to some civil statute violation and repayment to avoid receiving a felony conviction that could also cause them to lose their medical or other professional license.

Corporate integrity agreements

A provider that has committed fraud (or possible fraud) can sometimes still stay in business if they are afforded the opportunity to sign a corporate integrity agreement with the victim agency in which the provider has to implement and abide by strict policies and procedures to ensure that the provider won't go astray again in the future.

The following information was reprinted from the Health and Human Services (HHS), Office of Inspector General's (OIG) website in June 2015 and provides details about corporate integrity agreements.

> *OIG negotiates corporate integrity agreements (CIA) with health care providers and other entities as part of the settlement of Federal health care program investigations arising under a variety of civil false claims statutes. Providers or entities agree to the obligations, and in exchange, OIG agrees not to seek their exclusion from participation in Medicare, Medicaid, or other Federal health care programs.*
>
> *CIAs have many common elements, but each one addresses the specific facts at issue and often attempts to accommodate and recognize many of the elements of preexisting voluntary compliance programs. A comprehensive CIA typically lasts 5 years and includes requirements to:*
>
> - *hire a compliance officer or appoint a compliance committee;*
> - *develop written standards and policies;*
> - *implement a comprehensive employee training program;*
> - *retain an independent review organization to conduct annual reviews;*
> - *establish a confidential disclosure program;*
> - *restrict employment of ineligible persons;*
> - *report overpayments, reportable events, and ongoing investigations or legal proceedings; and*
> - *provide an implementation report and annual reports to OIG on the status of the entity's compliance activities.*

For additional details, visit HHS OIG's website: https://oig.hhs.gov/compliance/corporate-integrity-agreements/.

Author's Note: *This same website has a link to HHS's Exclusion Database, which is searchable by individual or entity name as well as other information of interest to healthcare providers and investigators.*

In summary, once the investigation and adjudicative action has been completed, the investigator usually has some additional work to do before the case file can actually be retired.

The next chapter provides a sample case study in which readers can get an idea how information provided in this book can be applied or considered after receipt of a complaint.

chapter thirteen

Sample case study utilizing "The Piper Method"

To illustrate how information and guidance provided in this book can actually be applied in the field, a fictional case study is provided in the following. Many healthcare fraud fighters serve as auditors, analysts, examiners, consultants, or in similar investigative-type positions, and very often their information is provided to field investigators to prove (or disprove) if fraud occurred or perhaps is still occurring. Many of the referrals end up in the hands of federal or state law enforcement investigators. In this sample case study, the fictional assigned investigator will assume the role of a senior federal agent that routinely investigates healthcare fraud. This sample case study will provide my personal insight into how an investigator (in this case a federal agent) might go about conducting a healthcare fraud investigation while utilizing *The Piper Method of Conducting Thorough and Complete Investigations.*

This fictional case study is intentionally written to serve as a less detailed overview of the previously described suggested investigative process. It does not include all possible investigative steps or details that would ordinarily be written in an official report to fully describe a complete investigation. As you may know, actual high-dollar healthcare fraud investigations often take years to complete. This is sometimes due to the assigned investigator's other responsibilities, including simultaneously investigating other existing unrelated cases, the opening of other new cases, participation in training, preparing for office inspections and supervisory case reviews, assisting other agents, waiting for supervisory approval of the investigator's drafted reports and requests, and waiting for others to complete assigned tasks, such as complying with subpoenas and so forth.

All names of persons, entities, agencies, and organizations listed in the following sample case study are fictional. Any resemblance of this case or individuals, entities, or others is purely coincidental.

Background information

The assigned investigator is Special Agent (SA) Joe Gumshoe. SA Gumshoe is employed by a federal investigative agency named the

"Federal Healthcare Fraud Bureau." SA Gumshoe was raised on the South Side of Chicago and has served as a federal agent for more than 15 years. He works in a small, one-agent office in Memphis, Tennessee. His immediate supervisor's office is located in Nashville, Tennessee.

The case assigned is a referral (dated January 10, 2014) that was received by SA Gumshoe (on January 14, 2014) from the program integrity office of ABC Insurance Company located in New York, New York. The referral pertains to a healthcare facility that provides outpatient psychological care in a building located in Memphis. The name of the entity is "Bee-havior Specialists," hereafter referred to as BHS.

The referral reflects that BHS appears to have used (and apparently is still using) lesser educated mental health providers (not doctors) to provide psychological care to patients that are covered by ABC Insurance. BHS's claim forms are signed indicating that the services were provided by Dr. Carl C. Crookmaster, BHS's owner. ABC's program integrity office previously sent three requests to BHS asking that they provide supportive documentation (provider notes) for the mental health services provided to 10 different specified patients during the past 12 months.

The referral includes copies of ABC's three previous requests for supportive documentation, which are dated October 1, 2013, November 1, 2013, and December 2, 2013. The referral reflects that BHS failed to respond to all three requests. The referral also includes a CD that contains an Excel spreadsheet that has data or information about BHS's previous claims submitted and paid for services said to have been provided from January 1, 2009 through December 31, 2013. Some of the more recent claims have not yet been processed. BHS was never previously investigated for any questionable claims. The estimated dollar loss is unknown. ABC Insurance Company has paid BHS the following amounts to date (some claims are still being processed):

- 2009: $400,200.00
- 2010: $700,400.00
- 2011: $850,600.00
- 2012: $950,800.00
- 2013: $1,200,000.00

Also included in the referral is a hard copy folder that contains ABC's paperwork on three known healthcare providers at BHS along with copies of their signed provider agreements. The provider agreements reflect that they agreed to abide by all of ABC's treatment claim submission policies and procedures when they accepted assignment into ABC's insurance program.

The three known providers are as follows:

1. Dr. Carl C. Crookmaster (owner)
2. Licensed Clinical Social Worker (LCSW) Nancy N. Nuts
3. Licensed Clinical Social Worker (LCSW) Peter P. Picky

Conducting the investigation

January 14, 2014

The Case Initiation

SA Gumshoe sits at his desk and opens the envelope containing the referral from ABC Insurance Company's program integrity office. He reads the cover letter and the copies of the three previous requests for BHS to provide supportive documentation. Gumshoe then reads the information in the three healthcare provider files. He glances at the CD but elects not to review its contents at this time.

Next, Gumshoe walks over to his copy machine and makes two copies of the referral's cover letter and the three previous requests for supportive documentation that were ignored by BHS. Sitting back at his desk, he turns on his computer and accesses his agency's internal intranet site to officially open a case and obtain a unique case ID number.

After obtaining the new case number, Gumshoe creates a new e-folder on his computer and names it "BHS." He then opens a Microsoft Word document and begins preparing an official case initiation report that contains the information about the referral. He includes as attachments to the report copies of the original referral and the three previous unanswered requests for supportive documentation.

After completing the report, he sends it via e-mail to his supervisor in Nashville who needs to approve the report before it can be considered final.

After sending the e-mail, Gumshoe grabs a brand new manila folder and puts a label on it that includes the case number and the name of the suspect entity (BHS). He uses a two-hole punch to put holes in the top of his official report and places the report inside the official folder. Not long after, his supervisor returns the e-mail with a PDF signed copy of Gumshoe's case initiation. Gumshoe prints the e-mail and the PDF document and places both in his official case file. Gumshoe then grabs an accordion-type folder and scribbles on it with a black marker, "BHS—Working File." He then tosses inside it the original referral documents, CD and envelope, and the extra copies he made of the referral and three requests for supportive documentation.

Drafting the Investigative Plan

SA Gumshoe takes out a legal pad and scribbles at the top, "January 14, 2014, BHS, Investigative Plan." Next, he starts brainstorming what he's thinking about doing with his new case. Although his original draft notes are sloppily written and in no particular order, he eventually uses a second sheet of paper and more formally documents his draft investigative plan. His investigative plan sheet includes the following notes.

Investigative Plan on BHS: January 14, 2014

1.
   a. Do a cursory review of the CD that was provided by ABC's program integrity.
   b. Query the National Practitioner Data Bank (NPDB) on all three providers to determine if there is any negative information on them.
   c. Check the Internet to see what information is available on BHS.
   d. Check the Internet to see what information is available on the three providers.
   e. Check BHS's website to see what's listed there and verify the address that the three requests for supportive documents were sent to. (Print or save the website as a PDF if it contains good info or photographs of any of the providers).
   f. Use *Wayback Machine* (http://archive.org/web/web.php) to review historic information on this same website. (It might identify previous providers.)
   g. Run a Dun & Bradstreet Comprehensive Report on BHS.
   h. Check online Tennessee Secretary of State Records on BHS and see if any of the three providers are associated with any other entities or if others are associated with BHS.
   i. Run social media (public info) searches on the three providers and BHS.
   j. Check online Tennessee state healthcare licensing verification for the providers.
   k. Run other online queries to identify assets, home addresses, cars, bankruptcies, liens, UCC filings, and so on, on all three providers, criminal histories (federal, state, and county).
   l. Do a covert drive-by and walk-by of BHS (take a few photos of the exterior). See if any provider and/or other business names are on the front door.
2. (*After I review the CD received from program integrity*)
   a. Inquire with other federal and state investigators and private insurance companies to determine if they ever investigated BHS or any of the three providers and ascertain if their insurance companies or government programs have also been paying BHS or any of the three providers. Let them know I opened a case and ask if they want to work jointly.

Sources for Evidence and Other Documents

- ABC Insurance Company (*any additional documents, policies, claims, payment info, etc.*)
- BHS (*everything*)
- Former BHS employees or providers (*take anything home?*)
- Current BHS employees or providers (*take anything home?*)
- Former and current patients (*EOBs, payments, dates of service; ask what provider they saw, etc.*)
- Other affected insurance companies (*if any*)
- Affected government healthcare programs (*if any*)

Investigative Tools to Consider

- Mail cover on BHS to possibly identify other insurance companies that are paying BHS and identify possible other providers or entities that receive mail at the same address. This might also identify the banks BHS uses.
- Trash cover on BHS—*Not needed yet.*
- Daytime surveillance on BHS—*Not needed yet, just the drive-by or walk-by.*
- Administrative Subpoena *(not grand jury) for all ABC Insurance Company patient and treatment records for past 3 years, billing records, Explanation of Benefit forms.*
- Grand Jury Subpoena *(perhaps later for bank records). Need to brief Assistant United States Attorney (AUSA)—Criminal Division first.*
- Search warrants (*not needed at this time*).

Interviews *(Not yet, later; also need to determine if any other investigators will be participating and if any other insurance companies or government programs were possibly victimized. Do this before conducting interviews.) Need to create separate interview packets on each interviewee and draft separate lists of questions for each before the interviews are conducted.*

Interviews to Conduct:

- If any new or former providers identified, do background queries on them and consider interviewing
- Former patients
- Current patients
- Former office workers at BHS
- Current office workers at BHS
- Licensed Clinical Social Worker (LCSW) Nancy N. Nuts
- Licensed Clinical Social Worker (LCSW) Peter P. Picky
- Dr. Carl C. Crookmaster (owner) (*interview him last*)

Possible Statutes Violated

Criminal Statutes

18 USA 1347: Healthcare Fraud
18 USC 1035: False Statements Relating to Healthcare Matters
18 USC 1956: Healthcare Money Laundering
18 USC 1001: False Statement (Oral, Written)
18 USC 371: Conspiracy
18 USC 286: Conspiracy Claims
18 USC 287: False Claim (does not have to be paid)
18 USC 1030: Computer Fraud
18 USC 1956: Money Laundering
18 USC 1341: 1343 (Mail and Wire Fraud)
18 USC 1516: Obstruction of a Federal Audit

Civil Statutes

31 USC 3729–3733 Civil False Claims Act

Prosecution (*later*)

- Need to brief Assistant United States Attorney—Criminal Division in Memphis
- Need to brief Assistant United States Attorney—Civil Division in Memphis

Additional Things to Check For

- Additional fraud
- Waste and abuse
- Systemic weaknesses and deficiencies
- Make recommendations for improvement (if identified)

Other Calendar Commitments

- My office will be inspected by HQ on June 13. I'll need to get ready the day before.
- I've got personal vacation planned July 3–7.

January 17, 2014

Review of Claims CD

SA Gumshoe spent several hours reviewing the CD provided by the ABC Insurance Company's program integrity office. He's concluded that it appears that Dr. Carl C. Crookmaster may have been signing all of the claim forms for the services that the lesser educated Licensed Clinical Social Workers (LCWS) may have performed. He's concluded this based on the lack of claims submitted under the names of BHS's LCSW providers. SA Gumshoe won't know for sure if that's what actually happened until reviewing the claim forms and the corresponding provider's patient notes. He knows that if that's the case, the patients would also be able to relate who actually provided their counseling sessions.

Call from Other Federal Investigative Agency

After reviewing the CD, SA Gumshoe received a telephone call from Special Agent Les Likely of the GGG, Office of Inspector General (GGG-OIG). SA Likely was raised in New York and has been an agent for 10 years. He informs SA Gumshoe that BHS has also submitted numerous insurance claims to GGG. SA Likely said he reviewed the claims data and it appeared that Dr. Carl C. Crookmaster may have been signing all of the insurance claim forms for the services that the lesser educated LCSW may have provided. SA Gumshoe jokes that he just did the same review of BHS's data and reached the same conclusion. SA Likely said he too will be opening an investigation. The dollar amount that GGG paid BHS is similar to the amounts paid by ABC Insurance. It was observed that the dollar amounts paid for the past several years have increased each year.

SA Likely asks if any other agencies or companies have been victimized or if any other investigators will be assisting. SA Gumshoe said that no one else has returned his calls or e-mails. The agents tentatively agree to talk again the following week.

Drive-by and Walk-by

That afternoon, SA Gumshoe drives by BHS's physical address and covertly snaps a few photos of the exterior. He later parks his car and walks closer to BHS front door but doesn't see any names on the door except the BHS name.

Mail Cover Requested

SA Gumshoe drafts a 30-day mail cover request for all first-class mail addressed to anyone or any entity at BHS's address. (The mail cover is subsequently approved by his supervisors and the U.S. Postal Service.)

Official File Updated

As the investigation progresses, SA Gumshoe and SA Likely provide each other with copies of their own agency's case initiation reports. SA Gumshoe placed a copy of GGG-OIG's case initiation in his own official case file along with copies of the mail cover request and approval. SA Gumshoe also wrote a short report describing his drive-by and walk-by and included copies of photos of the exterior of the building and placed the report in his official file. From this point on, SA Gumshoe always writes reports describing his investigative activity and includes them in his official case file. He also includes copies of any reports that GGG-OIG provides him with. SA Gumshoe also gives SA Likely copies of all investigative reports that Gumshoe writes. This way, both agents' official files contain most (perhaps all) of the same reports.

In the meantime, SA Gumshoe completes many of the things listed in Part 1 of his investigative plan.

February 28, 2014

Mail Cover Results Received

The mail cover results are provided to SA Gumshoe. They show that BHS is receiving regular mail from GGG and ABC Insurance Company. No mail was received from any other insurance companies or government programs. Several financial institutions have also sent mail but SA Gumshoe has no way of knowing if BHS has bank accounts with those institutions or if they were just junk mail. There's not much more useful information. SA Gumshoe does not copy the postal results provided because he's not permitted to. He returns the original mail cover results to the U.S. Postal Service as required.

March 3, 2014

Administrative Subpoenas Requested

SA Gumshoe and SA Likely agree to separately request administrative subpoenas from their own agencies requesting that BHS provide copies of all records of patient treatment (counseling), including counselor's patient notes, and claims submitted, payments received, and so forth for patients that had insurance coverage by their own organization's insurance company and government program. They also asked for the personnel files of all BHS employees for the past 5 years. Both will separately receive responses or results only for claims submitted to their own insurance company or program.

April 3, 2014

Both SA Gumshoe and SA Likely received their own agency's approval for administrative subpoenas from their headquarters along with the subpoenas to serve. They agree they will personally serve the subpoenas on BHS together the following day.

April 4, 2014

Subpoenas Served

9:00 AM: The two agents meet at Gumshoe's office and talk about the case for a while over a cup of coffee. They are both wearing suits and ties. They decide to drive their own government cars separately and to meet near BHS before going in.

10:15 AM: The two agents meet at and enter BHS. They are immediately greeted by a smiling receptionist who asks if she can help them. Both agents show their badges and credentials and ask to speak with the office manager. Looking startled, the receptionist calls out, "Stella! There are two federal agents here to see you!"

A few minutes later, a woman comes to the front and asks the agents if she can help them. Both agents again show their badges and credentials and state the purpose of their presence. The woman is identified as Stella Books. She said she was the office manager. The agents both serve Stella Books with their subpoenas and ask her to sign their receipts. Although hesitant to do so, she agrees and signs.

Stella Books asked the agents what the investigation is about. SA Gumshoe responded, "ABC Insurance Company previously requested that BHS provide supportive documentation for some claims. BHS never responded. So now we are pursuing the matter."

Stella Books then asks, "Both of you?" SA Likely smiled and replied, "Both of us." SA Gumshoe added, "You have 30 days to comply with the subpoenas. If you need more time or if you want to provide things in piecemeal, we'll be glad to stop by and pick up what you have."

Stella Books replied, "That's a whole lot of copying. I'm not sure how I'll get it done." The receptionist responded, "I guess I'll be working overtime." Both agents left business cards with the receptionist and Stella Books. SA Likely added, "If you need anything, call us." The agents left by using the typical police departure line of "Have a nice day."

After returning to his office, SA Gumshoe ran various online searches on Stella Books and found nothing of significance. He also updated his official file to reflect that the subpoena had been served. Not anticipating that many subpoenas would be used on the case, he opted not to create a subpoena log.

May 2, 2014

Subpoenas Compliance Extension Granted

Stella Books separately telephoned both SA Gumshoe and SA Likely and requested additional time to comply with the subpoenas. Both agents authorized an additional 3 weeks. SA Gumshoe updated his case file.

May 21, 2014

Subpoenaed Documents Ready for Pick Up

Stella Books telephoned separately both SA Gumshoe and SA Likely and advised that the subpoenaed documents were copied and ready to be picked up.

May 22, 2014

Subpoenaed Documents Received

9:30 AM: SA Gumshoe and SA Likely arrived at BHS and were met by Stella Books. Both agents were provided with six large banker's boxes each full of documents. Receipts were provided to Stella Books. Both agents carried out their own boxes of documents and transported them to their respective offices. SA Gumshoe updated his case file to show that documents had been provided in compliance with his agency's subpoena.

Subpoenaed Documents Inventoried

SA Gumshoe performed a cursory review of the documents inside the boxes and it appeared that everything was in order.

May 23–August 18, 2014

SA Gumshoe's had to prepare for his agency HQ's office inspection in early June, and the office was inspected on June 13. He went on vacation from July 3 through July 7 and worked on other cases too.

Subpoenaed Documents Reviewed

- SA Gumshoe wrote a report detailing the findings of his review of the subpoenaed documents. He found evidence that LCSW Nancy N. Nuts and LCSW Peter P. Picky were actually providing most of the counseling sessions, but all of the claim forms were signed by Dr. Carl C. Crookmaster. SA Gumshoe also found that numerous claims were submitted for services provided that were subsequently paid, but the patient files had no supportive documentation for those services.
- SA Gumshoe shared his findings with SA Likely who said he found the same exact things in the GGG files.
- Their review of employee files identified a former BHS officer manager. Her name was Tammy Truth who quit without notice approximately 1 year ago.

Saturday, August 23, 2014

Former Officer Manager Interviewed

9:30 AM: SAs Gumshoe and Likely arrived on the front doorstep of the home of Tammy Truth, BHS's former office manager. A woman answered the door and the agents showed their badges and credentials and identified themselves. After inviting the agents inside, Tammy Truth related that she previously served as the BHS office manager for over 5 years and that Dr. Crookmaster continually instructed her to complete all insurance claim forms with his own name on the signature block even though Dr. Crookmaster knew the actual providers should have signed the claim forms.

Tammy Truth said that the insurance companies and government programs paid a higher rate of reimbursement when the services were provided by a doctor as compared to lesser educated Licensed Clinical Social Workers. Truth said that she argued with Dr. Crookmaster several times about listing the wrong providers. She finally got fed up and quit because she did not want to be part of criminal activity.

When asked, Tammy Truth said she would gladly testify against Dr. Crookmaster. She said she did not know if the Licensed Clinical Social Workers knew what was going on and she did not possess any proof of any wrongdoing. She did not know anything about claims being submitted that did not have supportive documentation.

When asked, Truth said that she did not tell Dr. Crookmaster the real reason she quit and instead said that she wanted to spend more time helping her church.

The agents asked Truth if she would be willing to make a recorded telephone call to Dr. Crookmaster to see what he would say about his own knowledge of the false claims. Truth was slightly hesitant but agreed that she would assist.

The agents explained that they first needed to have their agency's approval before the call could be made.

August 25, 2014

Insurance Treatment Billing Policy Verified

Consensual Monitor Recording Request Submitted

After writing the report of interview, SA Gumshoe contacted ABC Insurance Company's Program Integrity Division that verified that they did pay approximately 10 percent more when doctors provided the counseling as compared to LCSWs. SA Likely reported the same about GGG's reimbursement policy.

Both SAs Likely and Gumshoe prepared their own interagency requests for consensual monitoring calls to be made by Tammy Truth to Dr. Crookmaster. The requests were electronically submitted through their own chains of command.

September 5, 2014

Consensual Monitor Recording Request Approved

Call Recorded between Tammy Truth and Dr. Crookmaster

9:00 AM: Both SAs Gumshoe and Likely's consensual monitoring requests were approved by their agency's headquarters. SA Gumshoe unlocked his tech-equipment locker and removed a digital recorder and phone patch. He grabbed two packs of new batteries.

10:00 AM: SA Likely telephoned Gumshoe and they discussed a strategy for a call from Tammy Truth to Dr. Crookmaster. Afterword, SA Gumshoe telephoned Tammy Truth and asked if the two agents could come over to discuss the possible recording.

11:30 AM: SAs Likely and Gumshoe arrived at Tammy Truth's house in SA Gumshoe's Government car. Gumshoe brought with him a small leather bag containing the recording equipment and a leather folder. After discussing a scenario for Tammy Truth to call Dr. Crookmaster, Truth agreed to place the call. The agents asked her to sign consent forms to make the calls showing that she made the calls voluntarily without coercion and gave her consent to record the calls.

12:15–12:45 PM: SA Gumshoe asked for silence as he turned on the digital recorder and recorded his own preamble by verbally providing the date, time, location, names of persons present, where the call will be placed from, where and to whom the call would be placed to, and who would be initiating the telephone conversation. Immediately after, SA Gumshoe dialed BHS's office telephone number from Tammy Truth's personal cell phone, and the call was recorded.

Tammy Truth spoke with Dr. Crookmaster on the phone and said that federal agents had just called her and related they were on their way over to her house to interview her about some false insurance claims that were submitted while she worked at BHS. Crookmaster told her to deny any knowledge. Tammy told Dr. Crookmaster that he was the one that directed her to keep listing his name on the claim forms even though he knew the lesser educated counselors provided the services. Dr. Crookmaster agreed that he did tell her to do that but said she should not tell the federal agents that.

Tammy added that he knew they improperly got paid extra by listing a doctor's name instead of the Licensed Clinical Social Workers' names. Dr. Crookmaster said, "Yes, I knew it was wrong and that we'd get paid more by listing my name. But I needed the money and you can't really complain because I paid you well." Tammy added that she was a religious person and didn't want to be part of anything illegal. Dr. Crookmaster said, "Just tell the agents you can't remember who did what. That won't be a complete lie because I'm sure you don't remember everything."

Tammy smiled at the agents knowing Dr. Crookmaster told all. She ended the call by saying, "Well, if they lock me up, I'll call you to bail me out!" Dr. Crookmaster laughed and said, "They won't lock you up, Tammy. Just tell them you can't remember everything."

Tammy disconnected the call and started to speak to the agents, but SA Gumshoe made a zipping motion across his lips urging her to remain quiet. SA Gumshoe then spoke into the recorder and provided his name and the time that that the call ended. He then turned the recorder off.

While still at Tammy's house they played back the recording for all to hear while everyone present smiled almost in disbelief in the manner Dr. Crookmaster incriminated himself. SA Likely said, "Now he knows the feds are investigating." SA Gumshoe said, "It doesn't matter. He's screwed!"

Before leaving, the agents told Tammy Truth that if Dr. Crookmaster called her asking what happened to just say that she told the agents that she couldn't remember everything—just as Dr. Crookmaster instructed her. The agents also asked Truth to document any future conversations she had with Dr. Crookmaster or anyone else about the fraud or the investigation.

Logging of Recording Evidence and Writing Reports

After departing, SAs Likely and Gumshoe stopped at a fast food restaurant and grabbed a bite to eat. SA Gumshoe carried the digital recorded in his jacket pocket to ensure the recording remained secure. They then returned to SA Gumshoe's office where he downloaded the digital recording onto his computer and made seven copies onto CDs. The first copy was secured as evidence and marked with Gumshoe's initials, date, and time. The first copy was then logged into his secured evidence storage room. Gumshoe gave two copies of the CD to SA Likely, kept two for himself, and placed the other two in his working file knowing that eventually copies would have to be provided to the federal prosecutors.

SA Gumshoe told SA Likely that he would write the report about the consensual monitoring and give Likely a copy. SA Likely was thrilled because he hates writing reports.

Saturday, September 6, 2014

Interview of Current Office Manager (Stella Books)

9:15 AM: SAs Likely and Gumshoe arrived at Stella Book's house and rang the doorbell. Books opened the door and asked, "Now what do you guys want? Can't you just talk to me at work instead of harassing me at my house?"

As a formality, the two agents again showed their badges and credentials and SA Likely spoke up, "We were just wondering if there was anything you wanted to tell us about. We assumed you'd be more comfortable talking to us here instead of at your office. If you'd rather we meet at our office or somewhere else that's fine too. Just let us know."

Stella Books then invited the agents inside her home and they sat at her kitchen table. She told the agents that the day before Dr. Crookmaster approached her after lunch and told her that there was a chance that some federal agents might try to ask her some questions and if they did she should say that they always typed Dr. Crookmaster's name on the claim forms because that's what we believed we are supposed to do it.

SA Likely asked, "Is that true?" Stella Books said that it was not true and that Dr. Crookmaster previously told her that they would make more money by listing him as the provider of all services instead of the lesser educated counselors.

SA Likely asked, "So you knew that submitting claims like that was wrong and you did it anyway?"

Stella Books replied, "Dr. Crookmaster said he would fire me if I couldn't do what he told me to do."

SA Likely asked if there were any witnesses to that conversation. And Stella said that the meeting was held behind closed doors.

The agents continued the interview for approximately 1 hour longer. She did not know anything about any claims being submitted without supportive documentation. SA Likely wrote the report of interview the next Monday morning.

September 8, 2014

Call Received from Defense Counsel

9:00 AM: SA Gumshoe received a telephone call from an attorney who said he represented BHS, Dr. Crookmaster, all employees and former employees and that no future interviews should be conducted of them without coordinating it through him. The attorney added that he would overnight write a letter reflecting that information to SA Gumshoe's office.

SA Gumshoe immediately notified SA Likely and his own supervisor about the defense attorney's call and wrote a report documenting the receipt of the call.

September 9, 2014

Agent Meeting to Discuss Future Plans

The following day, SAs Likely and Gumshoe met at Gumshoe's office and exchanged copies of reports that the two agents had written. They then discussed their investigative strategy.

They suggested that since they couldn't conduct any more interviews of employees, they could consider interviewing some of the patients to get them to say who actually provided the counseling sessions.

They predicted that none of the patients would ever lie if later asked which counselor they saw. Besides, the agents already had physical proof (the counselor's own patient notes) that the Licensed Clinical Social Workers did most of counseling. The agents decided they would wait to see what the federal prosecutors wanted to do about interviewing patients.

They also surmised that if the License Clinical Social Workers were later subpoenaed to testify at a grand jury, they would probably tell the truth too because they didn't seem to have profited from the scheme.

Both agents knew that they still needed to quantify the dollar losses by going through all of the claims and patient files and comparing them to the counselors' patient treatment notes. There were two types of false claims. Some claims falsely listed the providers' names on claim forms resulting in overpayments and some had no supportive documentation, which would be 100 percent false claims that should not have been paid at all. Technically, the entire dollar amount of any false claims submitted could be included because if any portion of the claim was false, the entire claim was false. They also realized that they might need additional proof to prove criminally (beyond a reasonable doubt) that the billing for services not rendered were false because they had no witnesses that could testify about that.

They elected to set up appointments to meet with Assistant United States Attorneys (AUSAs) from both the Criminal Division and the Civil Division and to present the evidence that they had thus far.

September 10–22, 2014

Audit Assistance to Quantify Dollar Losses

SAs Likely and Gumshoe both solicited audit assistance from the program integrity offices of their respective agencies that were later able to quantify the dollar losses.

Creation of Visual Aids

SA Likely spent a couple of hours making a few visual aids using Microsoft's PowerPoint to help when they presented their case to the prosecutors. One graph showed the total dollars paid to BHS over the past 5 years by both ABC Insurance Company and GGG. Another graph separately showed the dollar losses caused by incorrectly listing the higher educated provider who were paid at about 10 percent more per counseling session. Another graph showed the total dollar amounts billed for each of those claims. Another graph showed how much money was lost due to billing for services without supportive documentation. When all was said and done, the agents could prove the following:

ABC Insurance Company payments to BHS

Total paid	Total false claims
2009: $400,200.00	2009: $200,200.00
2010: $700,400.00	2010: $500,400.00
2011: $850,600.00	2011: $650,600.00
2012: $950,800.00	2012: $750,800.00
2013: $1,200,000.00	2013: $1,000,000.00
Total: $4,102,000.00	**Total: $3,102,000.00**

Note: Some 2013 claims not yet processed.

GGG payments to BHS

Total paid	Total false claims
2009: $401,000.00	2009: $201,000.00
2010: $701,000.00	2010: $501,000.00
2011: $851,600.00	2011: $651,600.00
2012: $951,800.00	2012: $751,800.00
2013: $1,201,000.00	2013: $1,001,000.00
Total: $4,106,400.00	**Total: $3,106,400.00**

Note: Some 2013 claims not yet processed.

- Combined total paid by ABC and GGG to BHS: $8,208,400.00.
- Combined total paid by ABC and GGG to BHS due in false claims: $6,208,400.00.

September 24, 2014

Presentations at the United States Attorney's Office

SAs Gumshoe and Likely met with the chiefs of the Criminal Division and Civil Division simultaneously at the U.S. Attorney's Office in Memphis, Tennessee. They presented their case, which included the use of visual aids, the playing of the recorded call from Tammy Truth to Dr. Crookmaster, and their verbal overviews of the information that both Tammy Truth and Stella Books provided.

They also provided each attorney with a binder that included copies of the following, which were individually tabbed and indexed:

- An up-to-date summary investigative report
- The initial referral from ABC Insurance Company

- Copies of the administrative subpoenas served and receipts
- All of the investigative reports prepared by both agents
- The audit reports that itemized and totaled the false claims
- Both ABC's and GGG's policies on listing the actual providers on the claim forms
- Copies of all three signed provider agreements from both ABC and GGG
- Samples of provider patient notes with corresponding false claims
- All signed documents pertaining to the recorded call between Tammy Truth and Dr. Crookmaster along with the evidence receipt
- Copies of the CD containing the audio recording between Tammy Truth and Dr. Crookmaster

Acceptance for Prosecution Consideration

Both the chiefs of the criminal and civil divisions accepted the cases for possible prosecution consideration. It was agreed that the assigned AUSAs would contact the agents to discuss future meetings and strategies.

September 25, 2014

Post Prosecution Acceptance Action

After the acceptance by the prosecutors, SAs Likely and Gumshoe knew there would be more work ahead. The criminal AUSA might call witnesses to the Grand Jury to testify and perhaps subpoena some bank and other records. The civil AUSA might want additional work done. Patients could also be interviewed. The case could easily go on for several more months.

Suspension and Debarment Considerations

Both agents provided their organization's program integrity legal counsel with copies of their summary reports to consider possible future suspension or debarment action against BHS or Dr. Crookmaster and asked that the legal counsel contact the assigned criminal and civil AUSAs.

Spin-Off Investigative Project Initiated

Based on their developed expertise into investigating psychological care providers for misrepresenting the actual providers of care on claim forms, SAs Likely and Gumshoe opened a joint investigative project in an attempt to identify other providers in the state of Tennessee that were doing the same thing as Dr. Crookmaster and BHS. The efforts would be coordinated with their own organization's offices of program integrity. Other insurance company Special Investigative Units (SIU) and agents from government insurance programs were invited to assist in the investigative efforts or future spin-off cases that were opened.

Deficiency Reports and Suggestions for Improvement

At the conclusion of the investigation, the two agents authored deficiency reports and provided written suggestions for improvement so that their organizations could initiate efforts to identify past and future claims submitted by psychological care providers for services rendered by lesser educated employees, but billed as if performed by higher educated counselors. One way would be to compare how many providers worked at the facility and to analyze the percentage of claims submitted under their names as compared to other providers who worked at the same facility. The reports and suggestions were provided to their organization's program integrity office and copies placed in the agents' official work files.

The above sample case summary provided a general idea how a healthcare fraud investigation may unfold using *The Piper Method*. It showed how the investigation started, how it progressed, and how it was presented for prosecution. Having a well-designed plan allowed the investigators to proceed like they had a road map. But as you observed, sometimes things develop that require a change of course. They identified an additional fraud scheme (no supportive documentation) while reviewing patient files. Initially, a consensually monitored and recorded phone call was not even on the planning list. But it was always in the back of the minds of the experienced investigators.

You observed that the investigators documented all of their investigative activity as they progressed and they shared their reports with each other. Reports included attachments that allowed the reports to be more informative. Evidence was secured and the chain of custody kept intact.

The agents knew that before presenting their case to the prosecutors that they had better have their act together. They obtained audit assistance and were able to quantify the dollar losses. Visual aids were prepared to demonstrate the dollar losses. Well-organized and tabbed binders were provided to both the criminal and civil prosecutors that contained just about everything the attorneys could want for future reference. The agents also played a copy of the audio recording that they obtained as evidence and provided verbal summaries of what the two witnesses told the agents.

The agents did not stop there. They notified the appropriate legal personnel within their organizations about possible suspension and debarment to consider in the future. They also wrote deficiency reports and made recommendations for improvement, which could possibly reduce future occurrences of this type of fraud or make it easier to detect within their own organizations.

Finally, based on what they learned, the investigators teamed together and opened a new investigative project in an effort to identify even more fraudsters that were doing the same things that they had just investigated. They were not selfish about what they learned either. They shared their knowledge with other healthcare fraud investigators and invited them to assist in the investigative project or future spin-off cases. They played like a team and used a thorough and complete investigative approach.

Conclusion

More can be done to combat healthcare fraud, waste, and abuse and to identify and fix systemic weaknesses and other deficiencies that cause or contribute to the detriment of America's healthcare system. Using the same ole' "whack-a-mole" investigative approach has been proven to be a less effective strategy that fails to serve the interests of catching more criminals, stopping wrongdoing, and/or improving the efficiency of the healthcare system.

Investigating only for criminal violations is insufficient. Every healthcare fraud investigator's objective should be to investigate for fraud, waste, and abuse and to identify systemic weaknesses and to make recommendations for improvement. Investigating only losses that meet an agency's high-dollar threshold prohibits investigators from making the best use of all available information, allows wrongdoers to continue or go unpunished, and often causes problems to escalate. Instead, I profess that we should strive to *Catch 'em all! Stop it all!* and *Fix it all!* Besides, it's a lot more fun fighting fraud with this approach.

It should be emphasized that most people that serve in the healthcare industry/profession are honest, caring, dedicated and committed to helping patients and have not engaged in any type of fraud. Many also perform and provide charitable work to assist those in need.

It's my hope that the information and suggested guidance provided in this book will benefit you and your organization. To those who continue to strive for perfection in this arena, I proudly salute your efforts and thank you for your service.

Appendix: Samples of healthcare fraud case presentation visual aids

SAMPLES
OF
HEALTHCARE FRAUD
CASE PRESENTATION
VISUAL AIDS

SAMPLE
HEALTHCARE FRAUD
INVESTIGATIVE
PRESENTATIONS

Fictitious Illustration Intended for Demonstration Purposes Only
Prepared by and photos by: Charles E. Piper, CFE, CRT

CASE PRESENTATION
VISUAL AID
Demonstrating
No Supportive Documents
for Healthcare Billings

DOCTOR I. DONTCARE'S
MEDICAL TREATMENT CENTER
MIAMI, FLORIDA

SAMPLE
HEALTHCARE FRAUD
INVESTIGATIVE
PRESENTATION

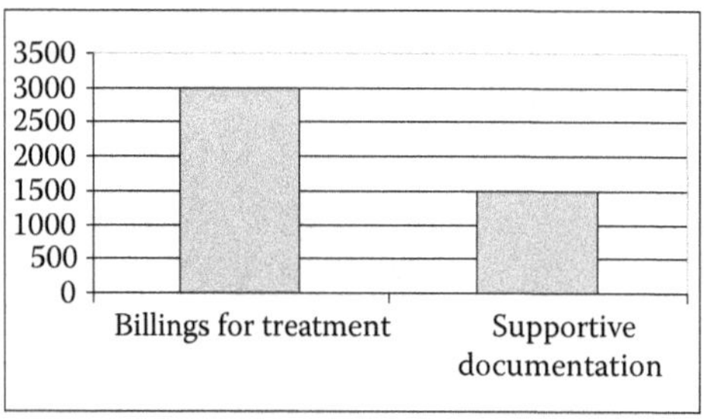

Time Period:
January 1, 2014
through
December 31, 2014

3000 Claims submitted
1500 Supportive documentation

Fictitious Illustration Intended for Demonstration Purposes Only
Prepared by: Charles E. Piper, CFE, CRT

Visual aid modified from Piper, Charles E., *Investigator and Fraud Fighter Guidebook: Operation War Stories*, (John Wiley & Sons, Hoboken, NJ, 2014. Copyright 2014, Wiley-VCH Verlag GmbH & Co. KGaA. Reproduced with permission.)

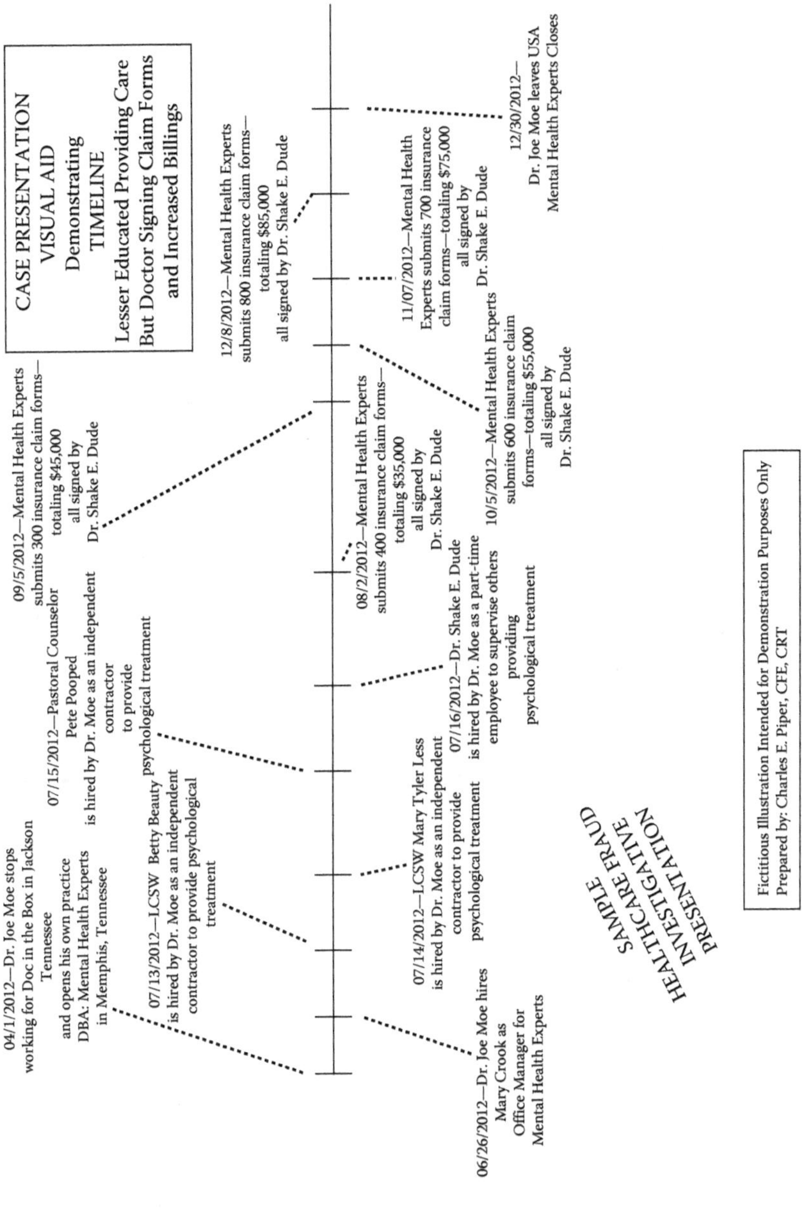
CASE PRESENTATION
VISUAL AID
Demonstrating
TIMELINE
Lesser Educated Providing Care
But Doctor Signing Claim Forms
and Increased Billings
04/1/2012—Dr. Joe Moe stops working for Doc in the Box in Jackson Tennessee and opens his own practice DBA: Mental Health Experts in Memphis, Tennessee
06/26/2012—Dr. Joe Moe hires Mary Crook as Office Manager for Mental Health Experts
07/13/2012—LCSW Betty Beauty is hired by Dr. Moe as an independent contractor to provide psychological treatment
07/14/2012—LCSW Mary Tyler Less is hired by Dr. Moe as an independent contractor to provide psychological treatment
07/15/2012—Pastoral Counselor Pete Pooped is hired by Dr. Moe as an independent contractor to provide psychological treatment
07/16/2012—Dr. Shake E. Dude is hired by Dr. Moe as a part-time employee to supervise others providing psychological treatment
08/2/2012—Mental Health Experts submits 400 insurance claim forms—totaling $35,000 all signed by Dr. Shake E. Dude
09/5/2012—Mental Health Experts submits 300 insurance claim forms—totaling $45,000 all signed by Dr. Shake E. Dude
10/5/2012—Mental Health Experts submits 600 insurance claim forms—totaling $55,000 all signed by Dr. Shake E. Dude
11/07/2012—Mental Health Experts submits 700 insurance claim forms—totaling $75,000 all signed by Dr. Shake E. Dude
12/8/2012—Mental Health Experts submits 800 insurance claim forms—totaling $85,000 all signed by Dr. Shake E. Dude
12/30/2012—Dr. Joe Moe leaves USA Mental Health Experts Closes
SAMPLE FRAUD HEALTHCARE INVESTIGATIVE PRESENTATION
Fictitious Illustration Intended for Demonstration Purposes Only
Prepared by: Charles E. Piper, CFE, CRT

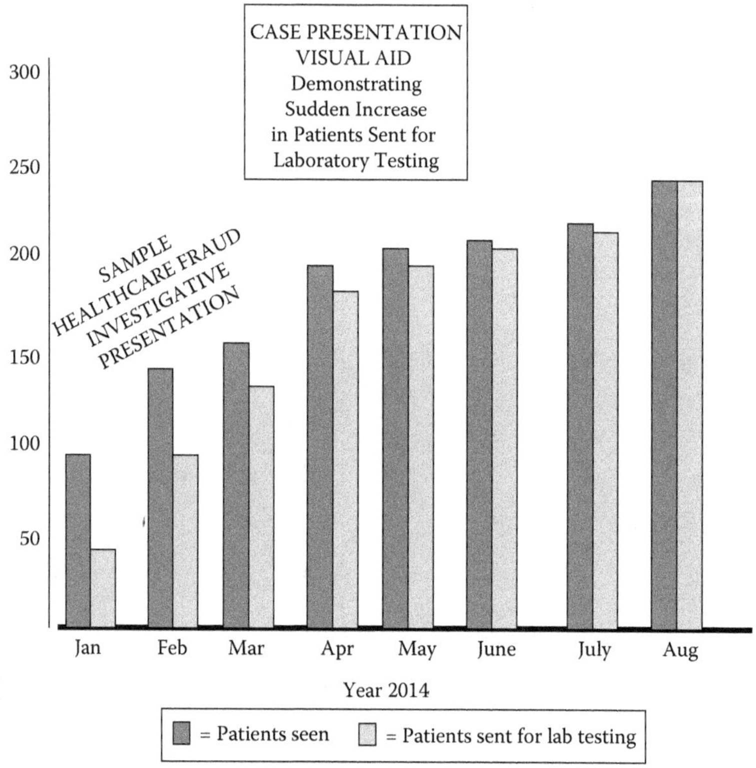

Fictitious Illustration Intended for Demonstration Purposes Only
Prepared by: Charles E. Piper, CFE, CRT

CASE PRESENTATION
VISUAL AID
Demonstrating
Patients Who Live
Outside of Florida
Regularly Prescribed
Painkillers
by Dr. Richguy
in Orlando, Florida

★ = 50 + patients prescribed painkillers in Orlando, Florida by Dr. Richguy in July 2014

SAMPLE
HEALTHCARE FRAUD
INVESTIGATIVE
PRESENTATION

Fictitious Illustration Intended for Demonstration Purposes Only
Prepared by: Charles E. Piper, CFE, CRT

1. 2/15/2012–3/17/2012: Dr. Miles in Europe
2. 8/01/2013–9/03/2013: Dr. Miles in Australia
3. 12/20/2013–1/02/2014: Dr. Miles in Cayman Islands
4. 3/12/2014–4/02/2014: Dr. Miles in Canada

CASE PRESENTATION
VISUAL AID
Demonstrating
Doctor Miles
was out of USA while reportedly
treating patients in Dallas, Texas

SAMPLE
HEALTHCARE FRAUD
INVESTIGATIVE
PRESENTATION

Fictitious Illustration Intended for Demonstration Purposes Only
Prepared by: Charles E. Piper, CFE, CRT

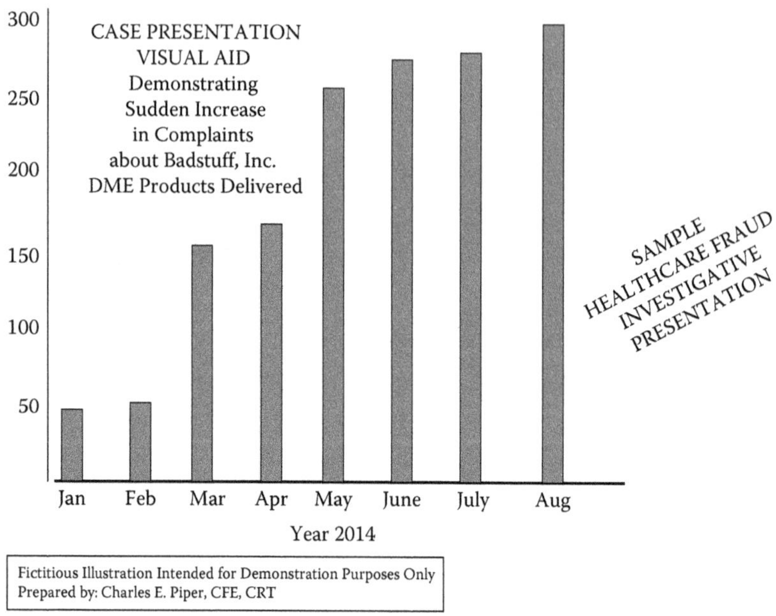
300
250
200
150
100
50
CASE PRESENTATION
VISUAL AID
Demonstrating
Sudden Increase
in Complaints
about Badstuff, Inc.
DME Products Delivered
SAMPLE
HEALTHCARE FRAUD
INVESTIGATIVE
PRESENTATION
Jan
Feb
Mar
Apr
May
June
July
Aug
Year 2014
Fictitious Illustration Intended for Demonstration Purposes Only
Prepared by: Charles E. Piper, CFE, CRT

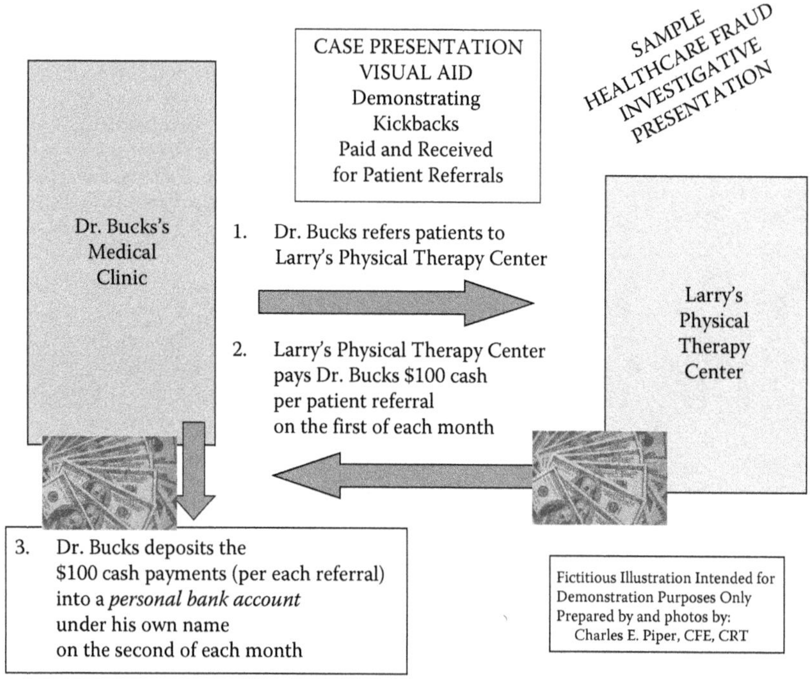
CASE PRESENTATION
VISUAL AID
Demonstrating
Kickbacks
Paid and Received
for Patient Referrals
SAMPLE
HEALTHCARE FRAUD
INVESTIGATIVE
PRESENTATION
Dr. Bucks's
Medical
Clinic
1. Dr. Bucks refers patients to Larry's Physical Therapy Center
Larry's
Physical
Therapy
Center
2. Larry's Physical Therapy Center pays Dr. Bucks $100 cash per patient referral on the first of each month
3. Dr. Bucks deposits the $100 cash payments (per each referral) into a *personal bank account* under his own name on the second of each month
Fictitious Illustration Intended for Demonstration Purposes Only
Prepared by and photos by:
Charles E. Piper, CFE, CRT

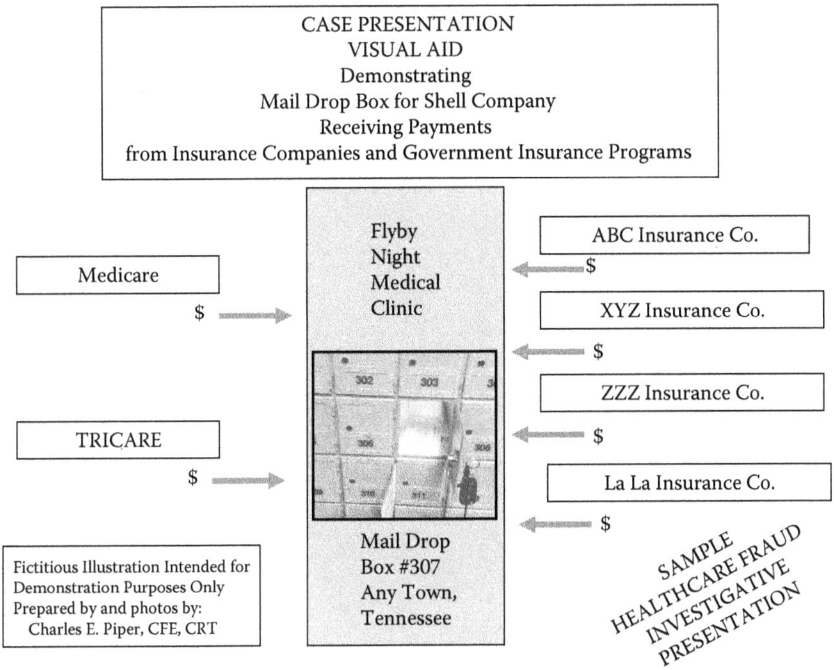
CASE PRESENTATION
VISUAL AID
Demonstrating
Mail Drop Box for Shell Company
Receiving Payments
from Insurance Companies and Government Insurance Programs
Medicare
$
TRICARE
$
Flyby
Night
Medical
Clinic
Mail Drop
Box #307
Any Town,
Tennessee
ABC Insurance Co.
$
XYZ Insurance Co.
$
ZZZ Insurance Co.
$
La La Insurance Co.
$
Fictitious Illustration Intended for
Demonstration Purposes Only
Prepared by and photos by:
Charles E. Piper, CFE, CRT
SAMPLE
HEALTHCARE FRAUD
INVESTIGATIVE
PRESENTATION

Index

For Product Safety Concerns and Information please contact our EU representative GPSR@taylorandfrancis.com
Taylor & Francis Verlag GmbH, Kaufingerstraße 24, 80331 München, Germany

www.ingramcontent.com/pod-product-compliance
Lightning Source LLC
LaVergne TN
LVHW021039011026
849160LV00008BA/554
* 9 7 8 1 4 9 8 7 5 2 6 0 2 *